Gaining Y
Interac

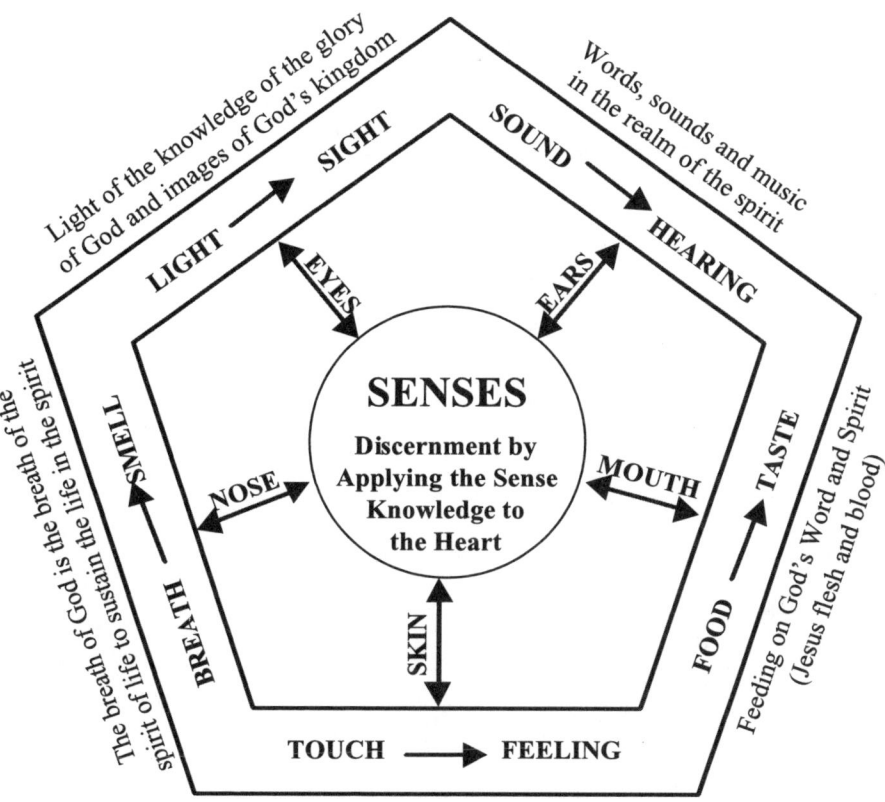

Gaining Your Ability to Interact with God

Dr. Caleb K. Kabilamany

Living Waters International Publishers, LLC
Lake Forest, California

All scripture quotations, unless otherwise indicated, are taken from the New King James Version. Copyright © 1982 by Thomas Nelson, Inc. Used by permission. All rights reserved.

Scripture quotations marked (NIV) are taken from the HOLY BIBLE, NEW INTERNATIONAL VERSION ® NIV ®, Copyright © 1973, 1978, 1984 by International Bible Society. Used by permission. All rights reserved.

Scripture quotations marked (KJV) are taken from the King James Version of the Bible.

Scripture quotations marked (AMP) are taken from the Amplified Bible, Copyright © 1954, 1958, 1962, 1964, 1965, 1987 by The Lockman Foundation. Used by permission.

Although author and the publisher have exhaustively researched all sources to ensure the accuracy and completeness of the information contained in this book, we assume no responsibility for errors, inaccuracies, omissions, or any other inconsistency herein. Any slights against people, places or organizations are unintentional.

1st Edition, 1st Printing

Gaining Your Ability to Interact with God
Operating Simultaneously in the Spiritual and Natural Realms
Copyright © 2002 by Caleb K. Kabilamany.
Library of Congress Control Number: 2002092520
ISBN 0-9721205-2-1

Published by:
Living Waters International Publishers, LLC
P.O. Box 1208
Lake Forest, California 92609
Web site: www.livingwatersip.com
Email: livingwatersintl@cox.net
Tel: (949)-215-0579
Fax:(949)-215-0498

ATTENTION ORGANIZATIONS, MINISTRIES, SCHOOLS, CHURCHES & BIBLE COLLEGES:
Quantity discounts are available on bulk purchases of this book for educational purposes or fund raising. Special books or book excerpts can also be created to fit specific needs. For information please contact Living Waters International Publishers.

Printed and bound in the United States of America. All rights reserved under international copyright law. No part of this book may be reproduced or transmitted in any form or by any means, electronic or mechanical, including photocopying, or by an information storage and retrieval system- except by a reviewer, who may quote brief passages in a review to be printed in a magazine or newspaper- without permission in writing from the publisher.

ACKNOWLEDGMENTS

Thanks to all those who attended my meetings including pastors, educators, leaders of various capacity, husbands, wives, fathers, mothers and children. Their hunger and thirst for God that manifested through their challenging questions motivated me to dig so deeply, to probe the entire Bible, to look beyond the readily available answers for true solutions. Above all, I thank God for the revelation, divine strength and resources that kept me going for several years without quitting.

I wish to express my special gratitude to number of couples and individuals who stood with me in prayer and helped me in various ways. They are Livingston & Sarah, Mike & Jasmine, Evangeline, Rev. Dr. Manuel, Rev. Wesley & Mary, Bonjo & Christalyn, Dr. Robert & Grace, Philip and David & Hannah. Moreover, without my wife Margaret and her untiring support this book wouldn't have materialized in this form. Cheering from my daughters Rebekah and Priscilla and consistent fasting and prayers by my brother Paul Paventhan and his associates kept my focus on the vision even in the midst of trying circumstances.

Dedicated to:

God the Father who enabled me to gain the ability to interact with Him in Jesus through the Holy Spirit . . .

my wife Margaret Premini and two daughters Rebekah and Priscilla who enabled me to effectively interact with ladies and girls . . .

my friends and relatives who enabled me to interact with you through this book, and . . .

my fellow citizens of the kingdom of God who enabled me to find a target audience to read this book.

Books by Dr. Caleb Kabilamany

How to Let God Flow through You
Living, Moving and Having Your Being in God for an Abundant Life

Accessing God's Goodness for All Your Needs
Living in God's Presence and Letting Him Restore His Glory upon Your Life

Gaining Your Ability to Interact with God
Operating Simultaneously in the Spiritual and Natural Realms

HOW TO CONTACT THE AUTHOR

Brief descriptions of the two of the three books listed above are available at the end of this book as part of the order forms. All the inquiries regarding the text should be directed to the author at the address below. Readers of this book are also encouraged to contact the author with comments and ideas for future editions.

    Caleb K. Kabilamany
    Living Waters International Publishers, LLC
    P.O Box 1208
    Lake Forest, CA 92609

    Web site: www.livingwatersip.com

    Email: livingwatersintl@cox.net

TABLE OF CONTENTS

List of Visual Summaries / Illustrations
Preface

Living, Moving and Having Our Being   15
    Make-up of Our Being   15
    Analogies for Our Inner Faculties and Functions   18
    Inner Desires that Drive the Life of Human Beings   22

Gaining or Losing Our Ability to Interact with God   27
    Salvation Plan of God for a Lost Humankind   29
    Freewill Choices and the Available Options   30
    Emotional Reactions for Various Issues of Life   33
    Gaining the Ability to Interact with God   34
    Losing the Ability to Interact with God Through Sin and Unbelief   38
    Eternal Destiny of Our Spirit, Soul and Body   40

Human Spirit Our Gateway into the Realm of God   41
    Bible References   46
      The Origin and the Immaterial Nature of the Human Spirit   46
      Character Attributes of the Spirit of Humankind   47
      Light for the Discernment by the Spirit   47
      The Human Spirit at the Death and Resurrection of the Body   48
      A New Spirit for Humankind Through God's New Covenant   48
      Receiving a New Spirit Through Repentance   49
      Nature and Character of a Newborn Spirit   50
      New Ability to Discern God and His Kingdom by the Newborn Spirit 50

Living the Life of God or Evil Through Our Body   51
    Bible References   57
      Body at Death and Resurrection   57
      Living the Life of God by Our Body Through a Life in the Spirit   59
      Life by God's Grace   60
      Living the Life of Evil by the Body by a Life Driven by the Flesh   60
      Evil Life by the Body Controlled by the Spirit of the World   61
      Casting Out Evil Spirits   62

Natural and Spiritual Discernment by Our Senses — 63
Bible References — 72
Inability of Humankind to Know God by the Natural Senses — 72
Eternal Life by Knowing God by Spiritual Senses and God's Spirit — 72
Sight: Eternal Life By Seeing God and His Kingdom in God's Light — 73
Hearing: Eternal Life by Hearing God's Word — 73
Taste: Eternal Life by Feeding on Jesus Flesh&Blood and the Spirit — 73
Touch: Eternal Life by Being One Spirit with the Lord — 74
Smell: Eternal Life by the Breath of the Almighty — 74

Saving of the Soul the Seat of Our Person — 75
Bible References — 80
The Soul of Humankind and Its Life in the Flesh — 80
Reactive Response of Our Soul for Issues of Life — 81
Destiny of Human Soul — 82
Jesus Saves Our Souls — 83
Salvation of Our Soul by the Word and the Spirit — 83
Forfeiting the Salvation Through Unbelief — 84

The Heart Our Inner Processing Center — 85
Bible References — 93
Heart Is the Central Part of Human — 93
Intents and Thoughts of the Human Heart — 93
Understanding by the Human Heart — 94
Knowing People by the Fruit from the Word in Their Heart — 95
Condition of the Uncircumcised Heart — 95
Spirit of the World in the Heart — 96
Holy Spirit in and Through Our Heart — 97

Regulating Lively and Deadly Thoughts and Intents by Our Mind — 99
Bible References — 104
Role of Our Mind in Storing, Recalling & Meditating Issues of Life — 105
Setting Our Mind for Team Work — 105
Futility of Mind that Does Not Believe in God Through Christ — 106
Life of God by Setting Our Mind on the Things of God — 107
Life of Death by Setting the Mind on Things of the Flesh & World — 108

Law Based and Love Prompted Conviction of Our Conscience   **109**
  Bible References   114
    The Moral Discernment by Our Conscience   114
    Day of God's Judgment in Eternity   114
    Conviction of Sinners of the World by God   115
    Inability to Redeem from a Guilty Conscience Without God   116
    Cleansing of Our Conscience by Jesus Blood   116
    Conviction of Believers' Conscience Based on Love   117
    The Conviction of Our Conscience in Various Scenarios   118

Bibliography   **119**

Index   **121**

Order Forms for Books by the Author   127

LIST OF VISUAL SUMMARIES / ILLUSTRATIONS

The Make-up of a Human Being	16
Analogies for the Faculties and Functions of Humankind	20
Desires and Motivations of Human Beings	24
Life of God for Believing Sinners	28
Freewill Choices of Humankind	32
Gaining the Ability to Interact with God	36
Character and Functions of the Spirit of Humankind	44
Occupants and Functions of the Human Body	56
Analogies for Sight and Hearing	68
Human Senses for Discernment	70
Living Conditions of the Human Soul	78
Role of the Human Heart in Character Development	88
Primary Attributes of the Human Heart	92
Three Different Settings of the Mind of Humankind	102
Conscience of Humankind Toward God and Others	112

Preface

We invariably discuss how God created us. However, the identity of and the distinction between the spirit, soul, body, heart, mind and conscience remain unclear to us. When sin infects our life and separates us from God, the way these faculties become dysfunctional is a mystery to us. In spite of this, we strive to make wise decisions by trying to discern the underlying motivations of people and governments. In other words, we get into a life long pursuit to find the right source of fulfillment so that the evil forces may not overtake us. However, we are often confused about finding ways to keep our heart with all diligence for the complex issues of life. We always wonder whether we can regulate our mind and conscience and get rid of those thoughts, which condemn us and bring us no edification. In essence, we seek to have some kind of control over the destiny of our life especially with regard to our spirit, soul and body.

If we love God in Jesus, the Bible reveals that God comes and dwells in us by His Spirit. For we will be born of God and receive a new heart and a new spirit. This new creature in us empowers God to manifest in and through us by the indwelling of the light of life, the spirit of life, the word of life and the love for life in Him. As a result, we can interact with Him and know Him and make Him the source of our life. Many practical aspects of gaining the ability to interact with God however puzzle us. Some of us ponder how God seated in heaven can fellowship with us here on earth and provide for all of our needs.

Analysis of these genuine concerns and the answers from the Bible are synthesized and presented in this book in an understandable format. Many practical, thought provoking analogies, visual summaries and illustrations are used. For example, the US president seated in the White House can manifest himself in a living room anywhere in the world through television. This is made possible by filling the space with the light of the knowledge of the images together with its animation, words and sounds via transmission waves. This kind of analogy is used to explain God's indwelling by the light, Spirit, word and love in us who are baptized (immersed and filled) with the Holy Spirit who fills the heaven and the earth.

In addition, components of equipment run by computers are used to explain the functions of the spirit. soul, body, heart, mind and conscience. While the soul is the operator who makes the choices, the role of the heart is compared with the central processing unit (CPU) of a computer.

The mind that sets the thoughts and intents of the heart is matched with a tuner or an icon. For a tuner selects a channel in a television and an icon loads and runs a particular program to the CPU in a computer. The conscience resembles an alarm system that activates the warning signals for violations. The spirit, our interface for the intangible realm, is likened unto the antenna / transmitter together with its interface of the equipment. The body, our interface for the tangible realm, is compared with the hardware of the equipment together with its interface that drives it. The soul, our life of the flesh that is in the blood, is likened to the life of the equipment that is seated in the electricity.

Analogies from modern technology similar to examples above are utilized to shed light on the way we can gain ability to interact with God. Since all of us have sinned and died unto God, we couldn't know Him. Jesus, being our sin atonement, became a life giving spirit to us. Now through intercession of Jesus, we can enter into God's presence and have a new life in the Spirit. As a result, we begin to interact with God.

Readers of this book will find personal guidance to save their soul and keep their body free of evil. When they are born again of God, the book will help them to recognize their newborn spirit and their new heart. They will be able to identify the underlying motivations of humankind and keep their heart with all diligence so as to lead an abundant life. The new ability to regulate their mind for edifying thoughts will empower them to make God the source of fulfillment for their desires. In addition, they may maintain a love walk with a clear conscience by letting God direct their thoughts, speech and actions.

The contents of this book are a cross between a friendly discussion of a slide presentation and a unique reference resource. Findings from years of research, meditation and development are simplified and presented in a discernible form to guide people from various walks of life. This is also a tool for teaching and word study for leaders and followers. Sermons, seminars and study materials can be readily prepared with little effort using the Bible verses, index and visual summaries included in this book. Bible verses pertaining to the precepts and claims by the author are reproduced at the end of most sections. College professors, pastors and other leaders can be tremendously benefited from the exposition of the information presented. Also, the word pictures may enable students and people who attend church to enrich their life with things of God. It will empower them to do the work of the ministry without engaging in years of rigorous training or personal study.

Living, Moving and Having Our Being

We may effectively handle the issues of life with a resolve that brings lasting fruits by understanding our make-up. The Bible is like the owner's manual from the manufacturer for humankind. It is like the mirror on which we can see our own image and know our face. Just as we cannot directly see our face without a mirror, we may not know our inner make-up without looking in the Bible. We come to know that God created us into spirit, soul and the body along with its senses, by looking into the mirror of His word. In addition, He gave us our heart, mind and conscience as an integral part of our being. The following description provides an introduction for the make-up of our being. It also includes the eternal destinations of our spirit, soul and body based on our choices in this life.

Make-up of Our Being

The *human soul*, which animates our body, is in the blood. When the blood is running through the body, there is life in its members. For the life of all flesh is its blood. The life is present when the blood is running through our body for: we see with our eyes; we hear with our ears; we smell with our nose; we taste with our mouth; we feel with our skin; we discern and store information with our brain and so on. The consciousness of our person, despite our location on earth now or in heaven or hell later, remains with our soul even through eternity. The proactive and reactive response ability, usually known as our freewill choices and emotions, are associated with our soul. In essence, *the soul is the seat of our person*.

We physically live our life in this world through the flesh and blood of our body. We live in this body by feeding on the daily bread and drink. The body is the interface to feed on food that sustains our life in this body. We even identify ourselves as separate individuals using our bodily features such as our face; color of skin, eyes and hair; height, weight and figure of our body. However, soon after our soul leaves the body (death), we cannot respond to anyone who calls on our name. For we lose our bodily ability to interact with the things of this world and its residents. Hence, our physical life is essentially rooted in the connection of our soul to the body. In other words, *the body provides our soul an interface to interact and sustain our life in the tangible material realm*.

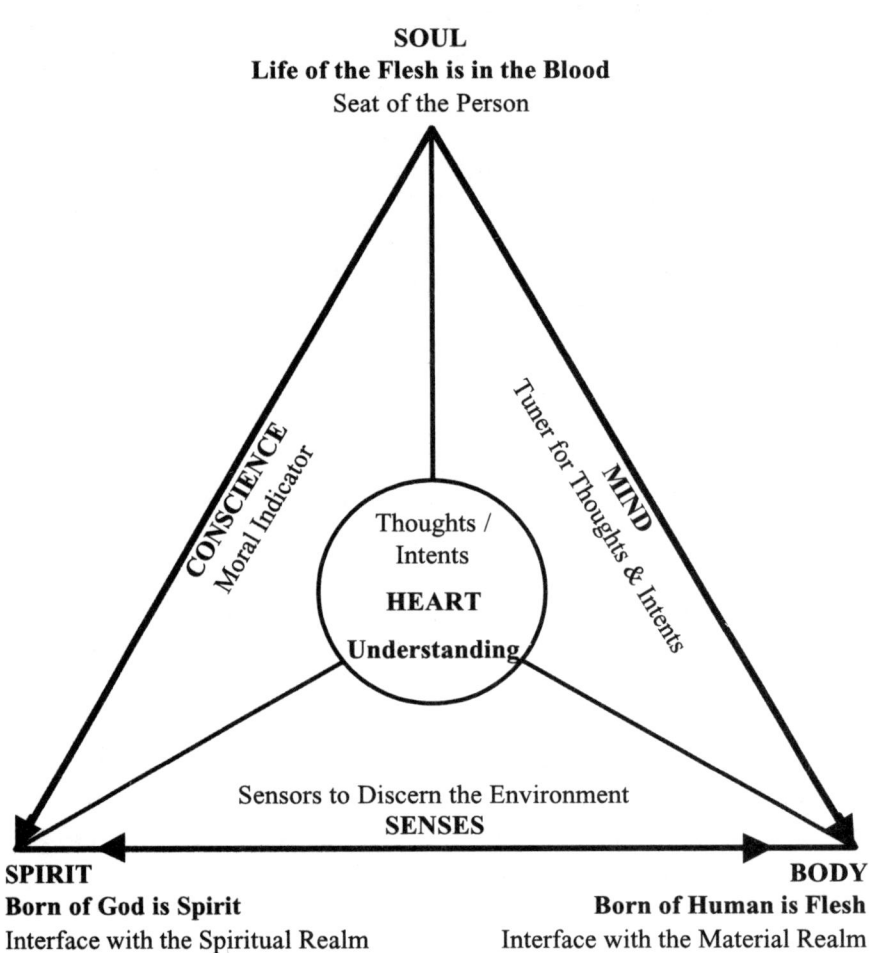

The Make-up of a Human Being

We enter and see the kingdom of God by being born again of God. God is Spirit. Therefore, that which is born of the flesh is flesh, and that which is born of the Spirit is spirit. The Bible says, man shall not live by bread alone but by every word that proceeds from the mouth of God. Jesus is the embodiment of the word of God. Jesus' flesh is therefore food indeed, and His blood is drink indeed. We who eat His flesh and drink His blood abide in Him and He in us. As the living Father has life in Himself, and Jesus lives because of the Father, so we who feed on Him will live because of Jesus. The physical characteristics of our body give us a separate identity from others in this world. Similarly, the characteristics of our spirit such as pride in spirit, humility in spirit, haste in spirit, calmness in spirit, spirit of fear, spirit of power, spirit of love, spirit of wisdom and understanding give us spiritual identity that separate us from the rest of the people. Moreover, we pray and worship God in the spirit. In essence, **our spirit is the interface to interact and sustain our life in the realm of the spirit where God is**.

The heart, mind, conscience and senses are also an integral part of our make-up. The **heart** is the central part of our inner person. We, by our soul, apply the knowledge gained through our spirit and body to our heart to gain understanding. We set the thoughts and intents of our heart by our **mind.** It helps us to reason in our heart to aid the process of understanding. In other words, what we are mindful of our heart at a particular instant is set by our mind. We, by our freewill choice, can set our mind either on things of God or things of the world or things of the flesh. Concurrently, the **conscience** bears witness for sin and righteousness, between two kinds of thoughts the one accusing the other excusing. It invariably shows the work of the law in our hearts for the moral issues of life. Natural and spiritual *senses* on the other hand, gather information around us and feed it to the heart for understanding. It aids us to discern our spiritual and natural environment, in which we live.

A visual summary of our make-up is presented on the page to the left. The soul, as shown at the top corner of the exterior triangle, is the seat of our person. It is the life of the flesh and it is in the blood. We, in our soul, react with our emotions and respond using our freewill choices. As shown by the arrows from the top corner towards the bottom corners of the triangle, we interface with the tangible material world through the body born of human and with the spiritual world through a newborn spirit born of God. The senses, as shown by the arrows along the bottom of the triangle, are seated in the spirit and body. We therefore discern our spiritual and natural environment with our senses. Also the heart, our central part, like a mirror reveals us. The mind that tunes our thoughts and intents sets the issues of life in our heart. The conscience, the moral indicator, monitors the issues of life for rightness. In essence, the issues of life that are lived out by our spirit and body, as shown by the summary descriptions inside the exterior triangle on page 16, are discerned by our senses and processed by our heart, mind and conscience.

Analogies for Our Inner Faculties and Functions

A word picture is used to enhance our understanding of certain functions of our heart, mind, conscience and senses together with our spirit, soul and body. For analogies in the word picture, various components of electrical and electronic equipment that employ computers are chosen.

The central processing unit (CPU) of the equipment sometimes receives and transmits information through intangible waves. It usually interacts through an interface that works with antenna and transmitter. The information that is transmitted includes commands from a remote source to execute certain tasks, light of the knowledge of the glory of images, words and music. Typical examples are TV, radio, internet, unmanned spaceships etc. The function of our new *spirit* born of God could be compared with the interface that works with antenna and transmitter. The Spirit of God carries information to us just as the wave transmits information to the equipment from a remote place. God's Spirit becomes the connection between heaven and us, if indeed He lives in us. We, in our heart (CPU) therefore, interact with God and things of the spiritual realm through our spirit. As a result, we may have the light of the knowledge of the glory of images, words, hymns and psalms and spiritual songs in our heart pertaining to God and His Kingdom. In other words, we become the dwelling place for the light of life, word of life, spirit of life and love for life from heaven.

The soul that is the seat of our person could be thought of as the operator of the equipment. When the electricity is turned on, the entire components of the equipment become alive. Similarly, life operation of our soul in the body is in the blood. Since knowledge accumulated through our physical and social lives cannot transcend beyond the tangible realm, the flesh and blood cannot inherit the kingdom of God. For eternal life is to know true God and His Christ. We have to be born again to see the kingdom of God. That which is born of the flesh is flesh, and that which is born of the Spirit is spirit. The physical body born of our natural parents provides us all that is necessary to interact with the material world around us. Simultaneously, the spirit born of God gives us the ability to interact with God and the things of His kingdom.

The hardware of the electrical and electronic equipment houses two kinds of life functions. The life of the equipment that is seated in the electricity and the life that is imparted by the incoming waves. Similarly, our *body* that could be compared with the hardware of the equipment also houses two kinds of life. The life of the flesh that is in the blood and the life according to infilling of the Holy Spirit or evil spirits. When we let our natural senses lead us, we may walk fulfilling the lust of our flesh. Alternatively, if we submit to evil spirits, they may possess our body and control us to live a life that is contrary to God. On the other hand, if we choose to follow the leadership of God in Jesus through the Holy Spirit, we will have the light of life, the word of life, the spirit of life and the love for life in us. God may empower us to overcome the flesh and evil spirits by the Spirit of God, who dwells in us.

Sensors used in any equipment such as antennas, microphones, cameras, thermometers and air quality monitors, essentially pick up the signals for images, words, sounds, temperature, air pollutants etc. Similarly our spiritual and natural *senses* pick up the signals from the spiritual and natural realms. They help us to discern the spiritual and natural environments, in which we live.

All the activities of any equipment are centralized in CPU. The CPU integrates the will of the operator with all built in requirements usually encoded in the programs. It coordinates and regulates all the activities of various components of the equipment according to the internal structure. The data from interfaces for various sensors, antenna and transmitters are applied to the CPU. It discerns them and presents it to the operator in an understandable form. The functions of our *heart* could be compared with the operations of a CPU. For example, whenever we want to gain understanding for issues of life, first we apply our heart to the knowledge and instruction. The issues may include the knowledge (*data*) from our natural and spiritual senses (*sensors*) to facilitate our reactive and proactive responses of our soul (*operator*). Then the meditation of our heart shall give us an understanding (*running the program*).

The heart also reflects our uplifting and wounding emotional reactions. The beliefs in our heart disclose the principles by which we live our life (*programs*). The values that determine our priorities on the

Gaining Your Ability to Interact with God

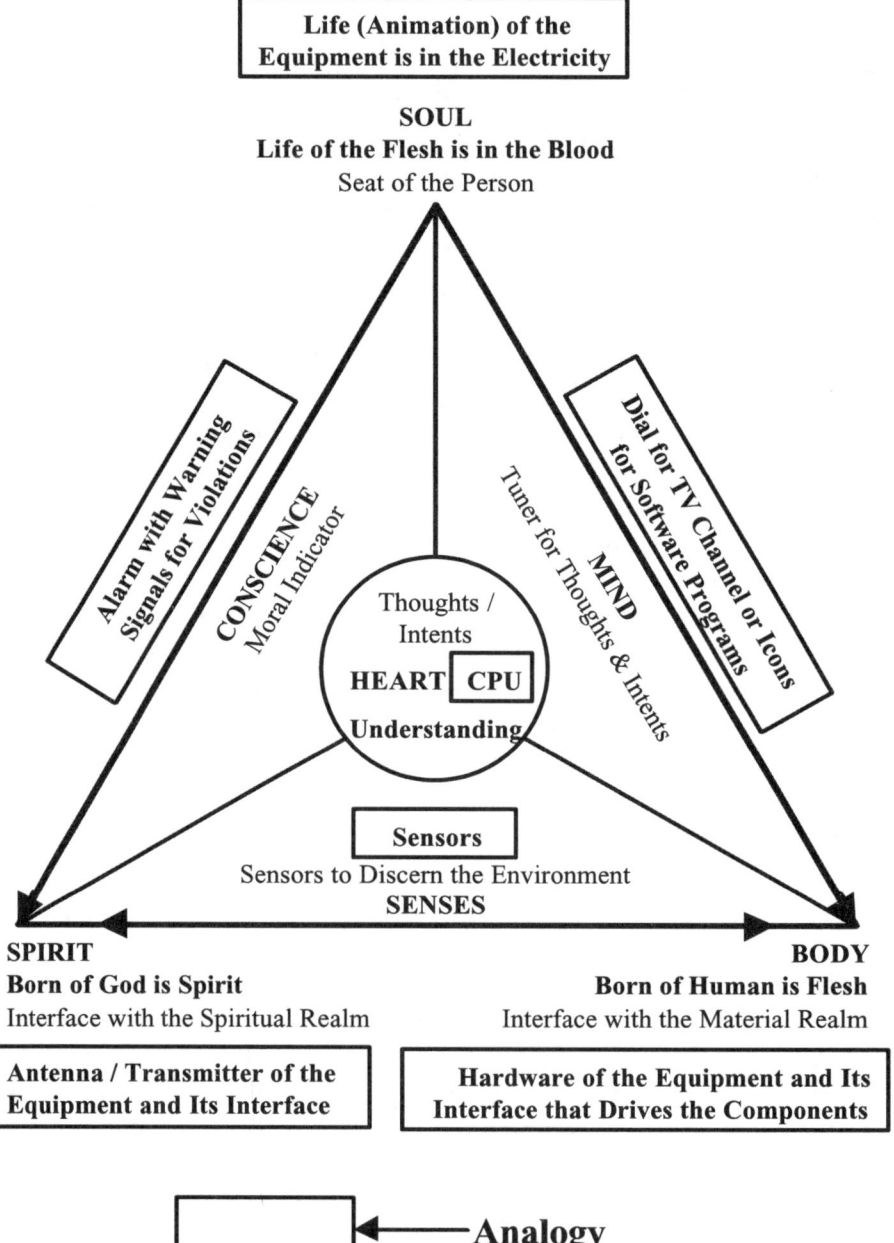

Analogies for the Faculties and Functions of Humankind

other hand show forth what we treasure in our heart (*organization*). We speak and do things out of the abundance (treasures) of our heart. This could be thought of as the output from the CPU through the speakers and moving parts of the equipment. In essence, as the mirror reflects our face, so our heart reveals us. What we think in our heart, so are we.

We use a dial and set a particular channel in a TV according to our freewill choice. Then the corresponding images, words and music fill the CPU and flow through the TV display and speakers in a discernible form. In another scenario, we load a certain software program of our choice in the CPU of a computer by clicking on an icon. The CPU executes a logical sequence of commands contained in the program on the data we input and accomplishes a certain task. The functions of our ***mind*** could be compared with the dial for the TV channels or icons for software programs. For example, if we set our ***mind*** on the things of God, we may be filled with the thoughts and intents in our heart, which pertain to God and His Kingdom. On the other hand, if we set our mind on the things of the world, our heart may be filled with the thoughts and intents of the god of this world, i.e., Satan himself. Moreover, if we set our mind on the things of the flesh, our heart may be filled with the thoughts and intents of the flesh that lead to death.

Now, we consider an alarm system of equipment that bears witness with every activity in the CPU. Whenever, activities exceed the limits set by the manufacturer the signals come on. We may have to call on the manufacturer to get rid of the error and the corresponding signals. The functions of our ***conscience*** could be compared with this alarm system with warning signals for violations. For example, our conscience bears witness with all the activities of our heart. It convicts for sin and righteousness and shows the work of the law in our heart. Once convicted of sin, the guilty conscience cannot be dealt with our gifts and sacrifices to God or people. We may have to call on the name of the Lord in repentance for forgiveness. For Jesus blood cleanses our conscience from all dead works to serve the living God.

A visual summary for the analogies in regard to the functions of our faculties described in this section is presented on the page to the left. The components of the equipment used for analogies are superimposed on top of the diagram for the make-up of a human being. The functionality of those components used for comparison is included within boxes on the left page, adjacent to corresponding faculties. As shown, the function of the ***heart*** may be compared with the operations of the central processing unit (CPU) of the computer component. The *mind* that sets the thoughts and intents of the heart may be thought of as the dial that tunes in the desired TV channel through CPU. The icons that load the specific software program to the CPU could also be compared with the function of the mind. The operation of the *conscience*, on the other hand, may be thought of as an alarm system that provides warning signals for violations in CPU operations. The *senses* that help us to discern the natural and spiritual environment are like unto various sensors that measure the environmental properties. The corresponding data is usually fed to the CPU (*heart*) for analysis and conclusions.

In addition, as shown on page 20, the function of our *spirit* may be compared with the activities of the interface that works with its antenna and transmitter. It helps the CPU to interact with the information in the intangible realm that comes from a remote source carried by transmission waves. The *soul*, on the other hand, is like the operator of the equipment. Moreover, the life of the soul in the body is like unto the life aspect of the equipment that is imparted when the electricity is turned on. Electricity plays a similar role like our blood that is the life of our flesh. The operation of the *body* may be compared with the hardware of the equipment that houses the interfaces for various activities and carry out the speech (speakers) and deeds (work by the equipment).

Inner Desires that Drive the Life of Human Beings

We have an inner desire to prosper in various aspects of our lives. It motivates us to develop love by faith and form right relationships with the Creator and His creation. For it helps us to make room to receive inheritance that fulfills our desire to prosper. We therefore invariably initiate and maintain relationships with God, other people, creatures and materials. For example, the children prosper by the grace of their parents by standing right with them. Similarly, the right relationships between husband and wife, owners of institutions and their client base, political leaders and their countrymen, employers and their employees, pave the way for prosperity. We also note that abusing people and other creatures and materials God has placed in this planet destroys our prosperity in the long term.

The grace to prosper may appear to abound from things immediately connected to us including people, organizations, creatures and materials. However, the source of grace that abounds in our life is God. It is appropriated through our right relationship with Him individually and corporately. This is like unto the water distribution system for a city. A house in the city seems to receive the water from a local pipeline. The water however is flowing from the reservoir (source) despite the complicated network of pipelines. If water is compared with the grace, reservoir with God, and the pipelines with other people and things, the analogy paints the picture how God's grace finds its way to us.

We may not be able to prosper in our soul if it is in bondage. We inherently therefore have an inner desire to be free. God is Word and His word is truth. The Word became flesh and dwelt among us as Jesus. If Jesus, the Son of God, therefore makes us free we shall be free indeed. The word of the Lord now is able to deliver our souls from bondage. When our soul is enslaved by sin, we may be operating out of a belief system contrary to the truth. If we however come to know the truth, the truth will make us free. The quest for freedom motivates us to develop a belief system according to the truth. When we believe and are baptized, we receive a new spirit, a new heart and the indwelling Holy Spirit. As a result, we will be able to walk in the spirit and inherit freedom. For where the Spirit of the Lord is there is liberty. For He empowers us to abide in God and experience freedom through His Son.

We have an inner desire to fellowship and worship someone or something in our lives. It continuously motivates us to develop knowledge about God and/or idols. For it makes room to arrange our priorities in our life so that God or any idol could be exalted and adored. This in turn quenches our inner desire to fellowship and worship. We, therefore, bow our knees and passionately devote our lives as a sacrifice either to God or to any idols as an act of worship. God is looking for those who worship Him in spirit and truth. We can be those people who are born again of the Spirit and the incorruptible seed, the word of God, and are baptized with the Holy Spirit. These people are empowered to fellowship with the Godhead and know the true God and worship Him in spirit and truth.

We have an inner desire to be valued by God and other people. It motivates us to develop a value system according to moral laws. For sin and transgression bring condemnation and devalue us in the sight of God and others. Our conscience invariably convicts us of sin and righteousness based on either the law of love or law of sin and death. We certainly get convicted when we violate God's priorities. For it introduces sinful idols in our life. We therefore strive to keep our inner peace by

Gaining Your Ability to Interact with God

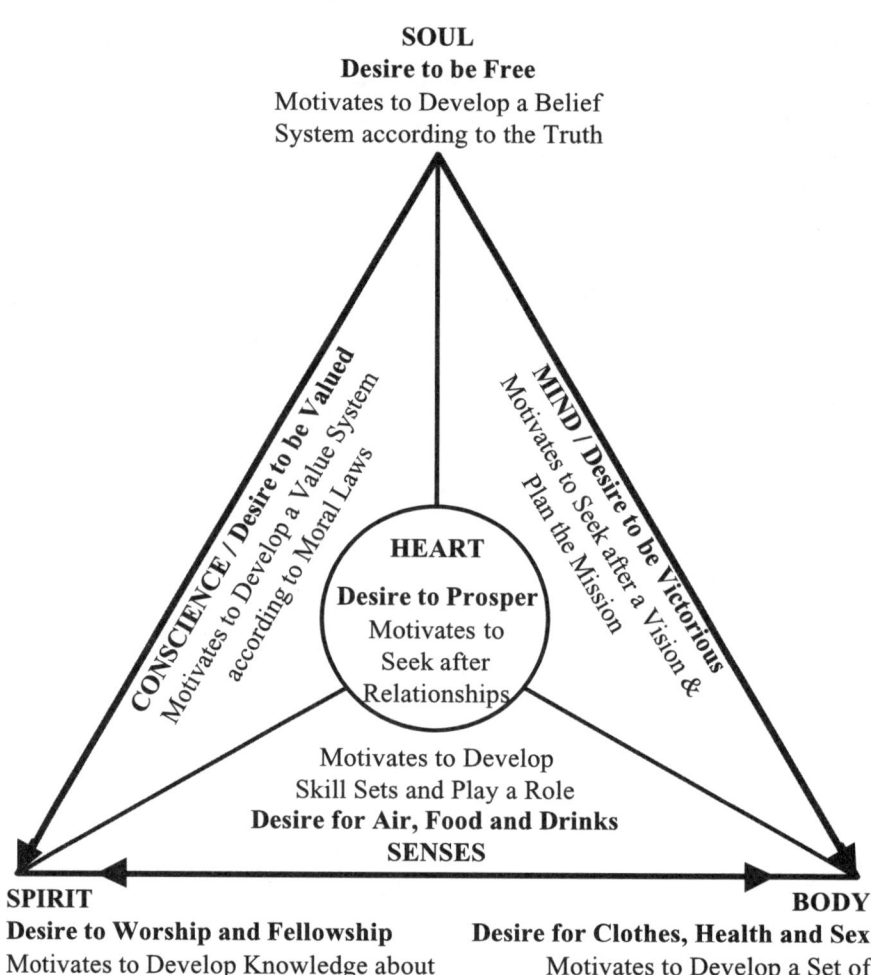

Desires and Motivations of Human Beings

living according to the conviction of our conscience. For it inherently fulfills our inner desire to be valued by God and other people.

We need air to breathe and food and drinks to sustain our physical life. As far as the life in the flesh is concerned, the natural senses help us to breathe clean air, and feed on healthy food and drink. On the other hand, in regard to our life in the spirit, the breath of the Almighty gives us life. Moreover, the word became flesh and dwelt among us as Jesus. We then feed on Jesus flesh and drink of the Spirit and Jesus blood to sustain our spiritual life. The spiritual senses help us to feed on these things to abide in eternal life. We have an inner desire for air, food and drinks. It motivates us to seek after a role in the society as well as in the kingdom of God for our life. For it makes room to live in an environment with provision that fulfills those desires. For example, we are assured of our provision when we play the role either as children for earthly parents or employees for organizations.

We have inner desires for clothing, health and sex. We therefore wear proper clothes and maintain our health for a sound physical life. We also get involved in sexual activities that multiply and sustain humanity in this world. The inner desire for clothing, health and sex motivates us to develop a set of boundaries for sanctification. We therefore develop skills and habits that sanctify our life for a mission. We choose clothing, food items and sexual activities within God given boundaries to stay modest, healthy and holy. There are numerous jobs we can pursue. Yet, we sanctify ourselves for a particular job. Similarly, there are many people who have the potential to become our spouse. Yet, we sanctify ourselves unto only one and carry out our married life. Living according to God's principles fulfills those inner desires without adding unnecessary troubles.

We have an inner desire to be victorious in various aspects of our lives. It motivates us to seek after a vision and plan the mission for our life by faith. For it makes room to fulfill our desire to be victorious. It may be noted that essentially all major victories of various individuals, as the history records, are faith or risk endeavors taken by men of courage. In other words, we plan and execute our life steps by faith and pursue the vision to reach our destiny that is our victory. Our mind therefore invariably sets the thoughts of our heart to overcome all obstacles that stand on the way to reach our goals. We, by God's grace therefore, run the race with patience and keep the faith to the end till the victory is won. For it fulfills our inner desire to be victorious.

A visual summary of inner desires common to humankind that motivate us to take various life steps is presented on page 24. They are superimposed on top of the faculties for humankind to enhance our understanding. As shown within the center circle on page 24, we have an inner desire to prosper in various aspects of our lives. The various desires that are shown on the visual summary essentially stem from this basic desire to prosper in order to have an abundant life. All faculties included on page 24 are directly or indirectly involved in handling every desire. However, a particular faculty, which involves the most in regard to stirring up or fulfillment of a particular desire, is matched on the summary. The various motivations stirred up by our inner desires are also included on the summary.

Gaining or Losing Our Ability to Interact with God

Adam and Eve, the first man and woman, sinned and fell short of the glory of God. Visualizing the scenario of their fall once again may help us to gain insight in regard to losing our ability to interact with God. The LORD God commanded Adam, saying, "Of every tree of the garden you may freely eat; but of the tree of the knowledge of good and evil you shall not eat, for in the day that you eat of it you shall surely die." Then the serpent (Satan) said to Eve, "You will not surely die. For God knows that in the day you eat of it your eyes will be opened, and you will be like God, knowing good and evil." So when Eve saw that the tree was good for food, that it was pleasant to the eyes, and a tree desirable to make one wise, she took of its fruit and ate. She also gave to her husband with her, and he ate. Then the eyes of both of them were opened, and they knew that they were naked; and they sewed fig leaves together and made themselves coverings.

We understand from the above scenario Adam and Eve ate of the tree of the knowledge of good and evil contrary to God's will. Consequently, they became conscious of sin and righteousness, according to the law of sin and death. We, who are his descendants also, like them show the work of the law written in our hearts. And, our conscience bears witness, between our thoughts accusing or else excusing us as guilty or not guilty. For by the law is the knowledge of sin. We know then that all the world becomes guilty before God. God in times past said that all souls that sin shall surely die. Sin that entered the whole world through the choices of Adam and Eve therefore reigned in death. The death spread to all human beings who descended from them, for all have sinned.

If we are dead unto God we do not abide in the light of life, word of life, spirit of life and love for life. For God is light; God is word; God is Spirit; and God is love. Our souls, being alienated from the life of God therefore, are in a lost condition in regard to God. As a result, we develop sinful beliefs and values that cause us to continuously suffer. We being the slaves of sin, let sin dominate our life through our will and emotions. Once we are convicted of sin, we do not have any inherent ability to redeem us from an evil conscience. Evil conscience continuously troubles our spirit that our spirit makes diligent search to find a way out. Since there is no way of escape without the mercy of God, our spirit invariably drinks in the poison of the arrows of an evil conscience.

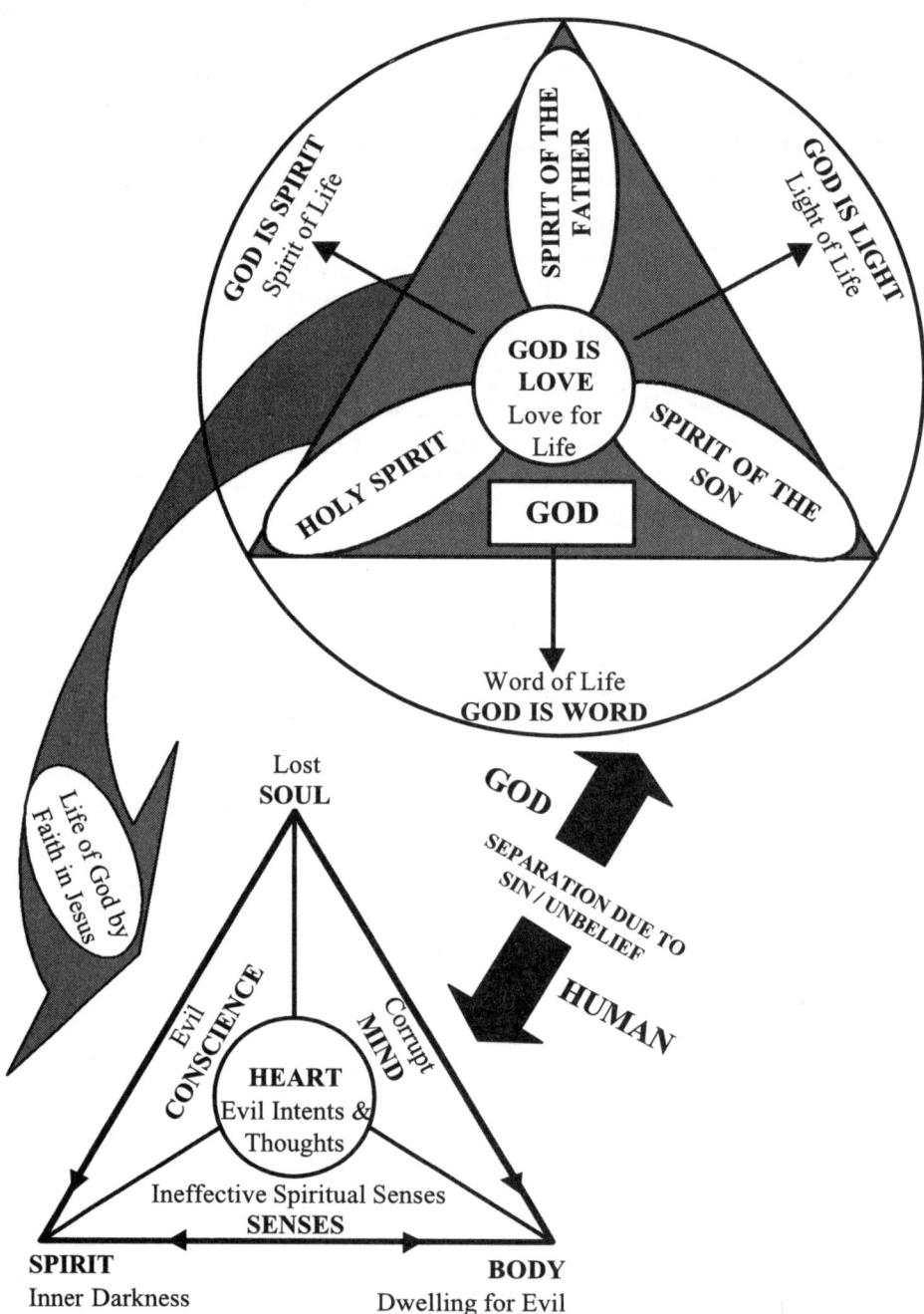

Life of God for Believing Sinners

If the light of life does not abide in us, darkness dominates our life in the spirit. As a result, our spiritual senses become ineffective to operate in the realm of God. We cannot know God or see His kingdom. Moreover, we are unable to abide in the love of God. This corrupts our minds and opens the door for the evil activities to dominate our life. For we walk either according to the flesh or spirit of the world. It is displayed by our walk in the lust of the flesh, lust of the eye and pride of life which are not of God the Father but of the world. Even, evil spirits may fill our hearts and possess our body. For we make room for them to exercise control over our life and get their will done through us.

Salvation Plan of God for a Lost Humankind

God however loved the world and provided us a way for salvation by faith in Jesus. For Jesus was our sin atonement who opened the gates of heaven for us to enter into God's presence that manifests through Spirit, light, word and love. The Spirit of God, who is with us now, convicts the world of sin, righteousness and judgment. Sin because they do not believe in Jesus, righteousness because they do not see Him who is seated at the right hand of the Father in heaven, judgment because the ruler of this world is judged. The gospel message of salvation in Jesus name is therefore preached to the end of the world through the Holy Spirit. God will eventually judge the secrets of people by Christ Jesus, according to the gospel. In that day, those who did not have Jesus, the sin atonement by believing and confessing Him as the Lord would be condemned.

A visual summary for the life of God for believing sinners is presented on the page to the left. The summary descriptions for the manifestation of God the Father, God the Son and the Holy Spirit are presented within the circle at the top on left page. The conditions of sinners or unbelievers are superimposed on top of the faculties for humankind and presented at the bottom of the left page. All aspects stated about sinners essentially stem from the lost condition of their soul as shown at the top corner of the bottom triangle. These people can have the life of God in them by faith in Christ Jesus, as shown within the curved arrow from top circle to the bottom triangle. The light of life, word of life, spirit of life and love for life shown within the top circle therefore will abide in believing sinners. This life in them by the light, word, spirit and love empowers them to interact with the fullness of the Godhead through the Spirit. A detail version of God's indwelling in believers of

Christ can be found in the book by the author entitled "How to Let God Flow Through You."

Freewill Choices and the Available Options

God has given us a freewill choice to be independent of His will or any others including people, governments, Satan and demons. It was evident by His non-interference when first man Adam fell by choosing to sin against the LORD. In addition, he is letting people, who freely choose to reject His redemption plan in Jesus, continue to live under the curse of the law. The curse may include eternal separation from God, sickness, poverty and the dominion of an evil enemy.

We make our choices according to our knowledge base for various issues of life. Thus, we may get destroyed in areas in which we lack knowledge. Alternatively, we can submit to a good knowledgeable leader who is able to direct our will, ways, plan and purposes that benefit us. Concurrently, if we do not resist evil leaders who control our will, by default, their will, plan and purposes may come to pass in our lives. Consequences of these choices are evident when we make long term commitments. They include marriage covenant with our spouse, work contracts with employers, voting for political leaders and covenant with God in Jesus. We keep these commitments by exercising our freewill choices to love and be faithful to our covenant partners even under adverse circumstances. In these cases, we freely choose to submit our will to others motivated by love, faith, hope and fear of God.

We essentially hand over the ultimate leadership to one of the three leaders who are usually identified as God, world (Satan) and self (flesh). If God is our leader, the Kingdom of God may be established in our life. For we let Him have His dominion in the affairs of our life by submitting to His will, ways, plan and purposes. On the other hand, if we submit to the spirit of the world, the kingdom of darkness will be established in our life. For we yield to the dominion of the god of this world, i.e., Satan himself. If we submit to the flesh, personal lordship will be established. For we want to dominate in our own affairs and be our own "god." Any kind of dominion outside God leads to destruction and death.

The body born of human aids us in fellowshipping with our natural parents through our senses, speech and deeds. Similarly, our new spirit born of God helps us to interact with the Father of our spirits in heaven. For we may be able to pray, worship and fellowship in the spirit with the help of the Spirit of God. While we speak, the breath creates the sound waves by the compression of air that transmits what we say or sing. In other words, we gain understanding for what is said by receiving into our ears the breath of the mouth of the one who speaks. Similarly, there is a spirit in us, and the breath of the Almighty gives us understanding.

If we have the Spirit of God in our heart, we can set our mind on the things of God and His Kingdom. As a result, our heart may be filled with the thoughts and intents that belong to God and His Kingdom. If we delight in the Lord and meditate long enough on those things, God may give the desires of our heart. In other words, we may know His will, ways, plan and purposes for our lives. Consequently, we may be able to submit to the leadership of God through God's word and the Holy Spirit. If we hear God's voice and see His glory and rule over our spirit in obedience to Him, we will display God's character. For we will be motivated by love, faith, hope and fear of God. Also, walking in the spirit enables us to put to death the deeds of the body by the Holy Spirit. If we therefore choose to lose our soul for God's sake, who does not control our will, we may lay hold of an abundant life. For we may rise to the maximum potential by following His leadership.

On the contrary, we may choose to submit to the leadership of the flesh by leaning on our own understanding. Motivation behind walking in the flesh is personal lordship. In other words, we keep the soul for our sake by setting our mind on the things of the flesh. If we meditate long enough on the thoughts and intents that fill our heart, we may be tempted. Let none of us say when we are tempted, "we are tempted by God"; for God cannot be tempted by evil, nor does He Himself tempt anyone. But each one of us is tempted when we are drawn away by our own desires and enticed. When desire has conceived, it gives birth to sin; and sin, when it is full-grown, brings forth death. If we therefore choose to walk in the flesh by fulfilling its desires, our life in the spirit will be made non-effect as a lamp under a bushel.

As another alternative, we may choose to submit to the leadership of this world according to its principalities, powers, rulers of the darkness of this world and spiritual wickedness in spiritual realm. We let the world control our will through oppression or intimidation or manipulation. Motivation behind walking according to the world is pride, lust, idols and fear of death. In other words, we lose our soul for the sake of the world by setting our mind on the things of the world. If we meditate long enough on the thoughts and intents that fill our heart, we may end up

Freewill Choices of Humankind

serving the god of this world. For we do not resist the devil who controls our will. We may even show spiritual attributes in our life in the spirit similar to Satan. Consequently, we let him minimize our potential in life through stealing, killing and destroying us.

A visual summary is presented on the page to the left for our freewill choices that drive humankind. As shown within the center circle, there are three major bases for our choices. They are summarized within three sectors separated by thick radial lines. The sectors reveal our three possible leaders namely God, spirit of the world (Satan), and us (flesh). The motivating factors for the choice of our leader are shown within the outer circular annulus on left page. The brief descriptions within sectors include the execution of our will to follow the leader of our choice in regard to our spirit, soul and body.

Emotional Reactions for Various Issues of Life

We may categorize our personal life primarily into three major parts to better describe our life into various realms. They are namely, the life in the flesh, the life in this world and the life in the spirit. We react emotionally in number of ways to our circumstances, as well as for various issues of life. If we are assured of an abundant life, the emotional reaction of our soul uplifts us. On the contrary, if our life is threatened by adverse conditions, the emotional reaction of our soul may wound us. We may choose to hide or expose those emotions of our soul through our spirit and body.

When the life in the flesh is under healthy, safe and secure environment, the emotion of our soul is serene like a calm sea. Feeding the desires of the flesh causes the soul to be satisfied with positive emotional reaction. On the contrary, whenever the life in the flesh is in jeopardy, the emotional reaction of our soul wounds us. The life-threatening conditions may include the activities of the enemies of our soul, sickness, dangers in child bearing, over exertion, extreme weather conditions and lack of food and drinks. The emotional reactions may be the way our soul expresses concern for those things that put our life at risk. The emotions may surround the issues such as enemies who seek after our life or a life of the loved one; ailment that results from sickness; weariness owing to stressful working conditions; fainting due to intolerable weather conditions; hunger and thirst due to lack of food and drink, etc. The soul, however, refreshes and quiets down when the enmity of others is dealt righteously, sickness gets healed and the body is properly rested and fed.

We live in this world primarily through our connection to the members of our society and the things of this world. Those who surround us may include the people from our family, birthplace, church, clubs, and places of study and work. Whenever, our status in this world is in jeopardy due to lack of approval or conflict with others, the emotional reaction of our soul may wound us. They include the concern for the opinion and dealings of others, economy and the political scenario. If the approval is gained or the conflict is resolved for the satisfaction of our soul, it quiets down. On the other hand, the ready approval of others stirs up uplifting emotional reactions of our soul.

Whenever, the sin is present in our life and our eternal life is in jeopardy, our soul reacts with wounding emotions. We therefore by our spirit search ourselves and know what is in us. For example, we examine whether we lifted our soul to serve or worship any idol. In case we sinned, the spirit enables us to know whether we received the mercy and grace of God through our repentance. Once the fellowship with God is re-established our soul quiets down. On the other hand, if we have a rich fellowship with the Lord by praying and worshipping in the spirit, the soul rejoices. For we invariably long in our soul for the Lord.

The body may act as an interface for us to express those emotions to other people and things of this world. Sometimes we expose those emotions through our body utilizing words and deeds accompanied by various expressions of our countenance. These may include contentment, smiling and laughter from a satisfied soul. We also express the wounding emotions through our bodily members. In this case, our words and deeds may accompany with sadness, weeping, screaming with facial expressions that manifest the wounded condition of our soul.

These emotional reactions of our soul may also be expressed through our spirit in various ways. When we are emotionally wounded, we have the spirit of heaviness. We sometimes get overwhelmed in the spirit and have a broken spirit. If we however rejoice in the spirit, we hold ourselves steady in life even under adversity and show positive attitudes.

Gaining the Ability to Interact with God

By the sorrow of the heart the spirit is broken and a broken spirit dries the bones. Who can bear a broken spirit? Surely, godly sorrow leads us unto repentance. We then pray like David "Answer me speedily, O LORD; my spirit fails! Do not hide Your face from me, otherwise I be like those who go down into the pit." The sacrifices of God are a broken spirit, a broken and a contrite heart-- these, our God will not despise. Blessed are the poor in spirit, for theirs is the kingdom of heaven. The LORD is near to those who have a broken heart, and saves such as those who have a contrite spirit.

God in old times spoke through His prophets and said, "Cast away from you all the transgressions which you have committed, and get yourselves a new heart and a new spirit. For why should you die, O house of Israel? For I have no pleasure in the death of one who dies. Therefore turn and live. I will give you a new heart and put a new spirit within you; I will take the heart of stone out of your flesh and give you a heart of flesh. I will put My Spirit within you and cause you to walk in My statutes, and you will keep My judgments and do them." We therefore can pray like David and say, "Create in me a clean heart, O God, and renew a steadfast spirit within me. Do not cast me away from Your presence, and do not take Your Holy Spirit from me. Restore to me the joy of Your salvation, and uphold me by Your generous Spirit." He who is joined to the Lord is one spirit with Him.

God said that no one uncircumcised in heart shall enter His sanctuary. We then have to circumcise ourselves to the LORD, and take away the foreskins of our hearts. Otherwise God's fury comes forth like fire, and burns so that no one can quench it, because of the evil of our doings. Now it is the LORD our God who will circumcise our heart to love Him with all our heart and with all our soul, that we may live. Under the new covenant in Jesus therefore, the purpose of the commandment is love from a pure heart, from a good conscience, and from sincere faith. Also, the circumcision is that of the heart, in the Spirit, not in the flesh. The law of faith in Jesus therefore enables our heart to be freed from an evil conscience to draw near to God. For we are washed, justified and sanctified in the name and the blood of Jesus and the Holy Spirit.

When we receive Jesus by faith, we become covenant partakers with God. It lets the Spirit of the Lord come upon us and the power of the most high overshadow us. We, as a result, will be born again of God and become His children. It causes us to receive a new spirit and a new heart. For God is Spirit and that is born of the Spirit is spirit. Moreover, Jesus baptizes us with the Holy Spirit. Consequently, we become members of one growing body that is the dwelling place of God in the Spirit.

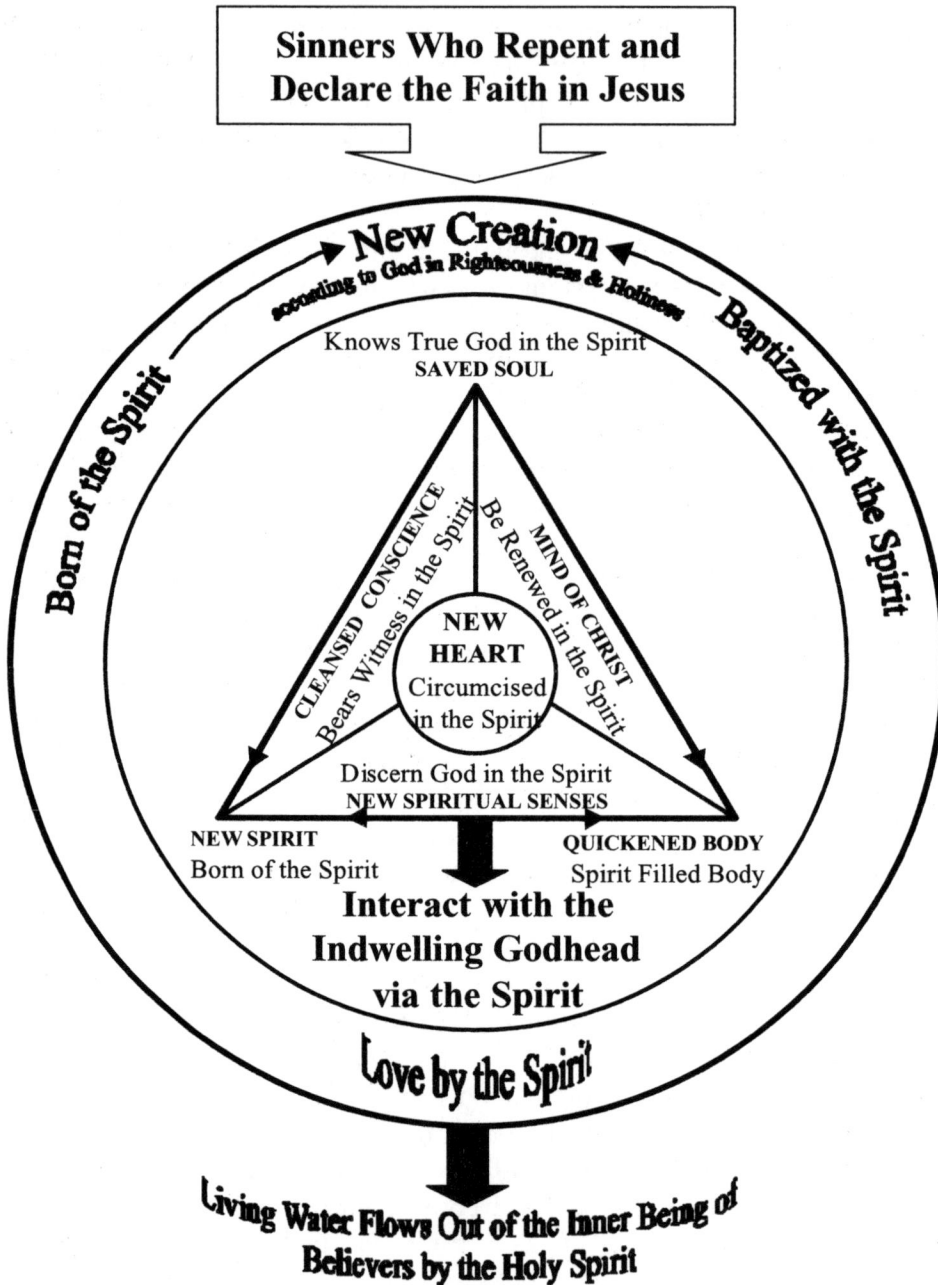

Gaining the Ability to Interact with God

Gaining or Losing Our Ability to Interact with God

Though all of us once got lost in regard to God due to sin and unbelief, God may begin to dwell in us due to our faith in Jesus. We who believe thus have the Spirit of the Father and the Spirit of the Son in us, if indeed the Spirit of God dwells in us. God is light, God is word, God is love and God is a Spirit. Consequently, we may fellowship with the Father, the Son and the Holy Spirit by abiding in the light of life, word of life, spirit of life and love for life.

We gain new spiritual senses due to our newborn spirit and new heart and the indwelling Holy Spirit sent from heaven. We will be able to see and walk in God's light, hear His voice, touch Him and taste Him. It empowers us to live in God's presence, fellowship with Godhead and know true God and His Christ. This new life in Christ lets the Spirit of God lead our thoughts, speech and deeds. Our conscience also bears witness with the Holy Spirit. We can be renewed in the spirit of our mind and have the mind of Christ. We will be empowered to make our bodily members instruments of righteousness and holiness. For we can put to death the deeds of the body by the Spirit of God. If we therefore yield to God's leading, we sow to the Spirit and reap eternal life. And, the living water shall flow out of our inner being from God, the source of our life. Consequently our soul, the seat of our person, no longer lives in a lost condition with respect to God and His kingdom.

The new creation may be compared with updating one of our electronic equipment that is run by computers. The new birth is similar to replacing the inner computer components such as CPU and interface cards, with new generation products. The external hardware and the operator however remain the same. The hardware and the operator could be compared with our body and soul, respectively. Installing a new CPU with loaded programs is like getting a new heart with laws written in it. Inserting an interface card to receive and transmit remote information is similar to receiving a new spirit. Baptism with the Spirit may be thought of as immersing the electronic equipment into the influence zone of intangible transmission waves. This empowers us to have life activities with anyone of our choice anywhere in the world. For example, the CPU can execute (thoughts), the speakers can broadcast (speech) and moving parts can carry out (deeds) things both from remote and local sources. Radio, TV, fax, internet system, communication satellite and unmanned spaceship are some examples of electronic equipment that help us to interact with people in remote places. Subsequently, the will, ways, plan and purposes of another person (God) can manifest in our life. For the new equipment helps us to know and agree with another person on the other end of our communication.

A visual summary for gaining the ability to interact with God is presented on page 36. As shown within the top box arrow, we who repent of our sin and declare our faith in Jesus are the ones who gain the ability to interact with God. For we submit to the Lordship of Jesus and are born of the Spirit and baptized with the Holy Spirit. Consequently, as described within the outer circular annulus on page 36, we are a new creation according to God in righteousness and holiness. We may have characteristics as described below.

The baptism with the Spirit enables our thoughts, speech and deeds to be directed by God. We may know God's will, ways, plan and purposes in our heart by the Spirit. A visual summary of the new creature is presented within the integrated triangles with a center circle at the middle of the diagram on page 36. As shown, by the indwelling Spirit of God we will have: a new spirit born of the Spirit, a new heart circumcised in the Spirit, cleansed conscience that bears witness in the Spirit and a Spirit filled body. Hence, we have new spiritual senses to discern God in the Spirit. We have the mind of Christ by being able to be renewed in the Spirit of our mind. Our souls therefore are no longer lost but saved and know true God in the Spirit.

When we live in the Spirit, as shown by an arrow at the bottom of the exterior triangle on page 36, we may be able to interact with Godhead who dwells in us. In many occasions, we do not know what we should pray for as we ought. The Spirit Himself helps in our weaknesses and makes intercession for us with groanings which cannot be uttered. Now we who search the hearts know what the mind of the Spirit is, because He makes intercession for the saints according to the will of God. When we yield to the love by the Spirit, as shown by an arrow at the bottom of the exterior circle on page 36, the living water shall flow out of our inner being by the Spirit of God. For God is the fountain of living waters. In essence, we can put on the new man, and interact with God and have a life in Him.

Losing the Ability to Interact with God Through Sin and Unbelief

Satan, who is an offense to God, is not mindful of the things of God, but the things of men. As the serpent deceived Eve by his craftiness, so the minds of hearers of the gospel may also be corrupted from the simplicity that is in Christ Jesus. Many do not enter in because of an evil heart of unbelief. For the god of this age has blinded their minds that the light of the gospel of the glory of Christ, who is the image of God, should not shine on them. To those who are defiled and unbelieving nothing is pure; but even their mind and conscience are defiled. They refuse to hear the law of faith in Christ and the words, which the LORD of hosts had sent by His Spirit through the former prophets and His Son.

Since God's righteousness is by faith, anything not of faith is sin. Many depart from the faith by giving heed to deceiving spirits and doctrines of demons. For they let Satan, father of lies, fill their hearts to lie to the Holy Spirit. They speak lies in hypocrisy, having their own conscience seared with a hot iron. Surely, they resist the truth, people of corrupt minds, disapproved concerning the faith. Being destitute of the truth, their minds are blinded. Although they knew God, they did not glorify Him as God, nor were thankful. They became futile in their thoughts, and their foolish hearts were darkened. They have a heart trained in covetous practices and exchange the truth of God for the lie. Professing to be wise, they become fools, and worship and serve the creature rather than the Creator.

Yes, they make their hearts like flint for they get hardened through the deceitfulness of sin. They become proud and have deceit in their spirit. A haughty spirit goes before a fall. Those who are stubborn and rebellious do not set their heart aright, and their spirit is not faithful to God. They get angry in their bosom and exalt folly by hastening in their spirit. They also may have a perverse tongue owing to a breach in the spirit. In this way, they surely depart from the living God.

Then the LORD sees their wickedness, for every intent of the thoughts of their hearts is only continually evil. Their heart gets lifted up, and their spirit is hardened in pride. Who has hardened himself against God and prospered? God indeed resists the proud and scatters them in the imagination of their hearts. In accordance with their hardness and their impenitent heart, they are treasuring up for themselves wrath. They will know their condition in the day of wrath and revelation of the righteous judgment of God.

They having their understanding darkened, being alienated from the life of God, because of the ignorance that is in them, because of the hardening of their heart, walk in the futility of their mind. For they did not like to retain God in their knowledge. They walk according to the course of this world, according to the prince of the power of the air, the spirit who now works in the sons of disobedience. Therefore, God gave them over to a debased mind, to do those things, which are not fitting. In other words, He gave them up to uncleanness, in the lusts of their hearts, to dishonor their bodies among themselves. Consequently, they conduct themselves in the lusts of their flesh, fulfilling the desires of the flesh and of the mind, and were by nature children of wrath.

The flesh and blood neither reveal the things of God nor inherit the kingdom of God. Also, corruption neither inherits incorruption. Out of the abundance of the heart the mouth speaks. An evil person out of the evil treasure of the heart brings forth evil things. Yet, everyone of them must appear before the judgment seat of Christ. All of them would give account on the day of judgment for every idle word they spoke. And, by their words they will be condemned. In addition, each one will receive the things done in the body, according to what he has done, whether good or bad. In essence, the dead will be judged according to their words and works, and those who are not in Christ will be condemned.

Eternal Destiny of Our Spirit, Soul and Body

Now, we consider the destiny of our spirit, soul and body. Sin entered the world and brought death to all humankind. Sin hardens the spirit and the heart like stone that sinners lose their sensitiveness or cease to be faithful to God. They lose their ability to know God or respond to the inspiration (call) of God despite the existence of their spirit. In other words, while they are alive in the flesh to others for a period of time, they are dead unto God. Their soul is in a lost condition in regard to God and His kingdom. This can be compared with the condition soon after the physical death of people. For they stop responding to the call of others, though their body is intact and left behind in this world.

Once the soul departs from the body on the day of death, the dust (body) will return to the earth as it was, and the spirit will return to God who gave it. All of us sinned and died once unto God. If we do not believe in the redemption plan of God by faith in Jesus, God will destroy our soul in hell. On the contrary, if we atone for our sin by our faith in Jesus name and blood, God is able to save our soul. For He will give us a new spirit and a new heart and put His Spirit within us. We will therefore know Him and walk with Him. He will also clothe us with a new heavenly body on the day of resurrection.

Human Spirit Our Gateway into the Realm of God

The Spirit of God has made us and breath of the Almighty gives us life. This was evident when LORD God formed the first man Adam out of the dust of the ground. He breathed into his nostrils the spirit of life and he became a living being. Moreover, all of the hosts of heavens were made by the breath of God's mouth.

Despite God's plan for humankind to prosper in Him, sin entered the world through first man Adam, and death through sin. Thus, death spread to all humankind, because all sinned. If God therefore should set His heart and gather to Himself His Spirit and His breath, all flesh should perish together and all of us would return to dust. Verily, the body without the spirit is dead. On the day of our death the spirit will return to God who gave it and the body (dust) will return to the earth as it was. No one indeed has power over the spirit to retain the spirit and no one has power in the day of death. However, when God resurrects the body the spirit returns, similar to the resurrection of some dead people during Jesus' earthly ministry.

God so loved the world that He gave His only begotten Son that whoever believes in Him should not perish, but have everlasting life. God is a Spirit and also Father of spirits. According to God's will, we who abide in death in regard to God can be born of God by faith in Jesus. We may note that which is born of the flesh is flesh and that which is born of the Spirit is spirit. A spirit does not have flesh and bones like our body that is born of our natural parents. In addition, God the Father and the Son dwell in us through the Holy Spirit owing to our faithfulness to God in Jesus through the new covenant. God the Father has life in Himself. Since, Father is in Jesus and Jesus is in the Father and Jesus is in us and we are in Jesus, Jesus is an intercessor for the life of God to abide in us. In other words, God the Father is the source of our life. And we, who have eternal life therefore, live, move and have our being in Him through Jesus and the Holy Spirit.

If we therefore are born again of God and receive a new spirit, our new man is created after God's righteousness and holiness. We may be able to live our life according to what we see in the kingdom of God. Sin may not have dominion over us since we do not live under law but under the grace and mercy of God. As a result, we can choose to walk in the spirit and overcome the flesh and the world.

Gaining Your Ability to Interact with God

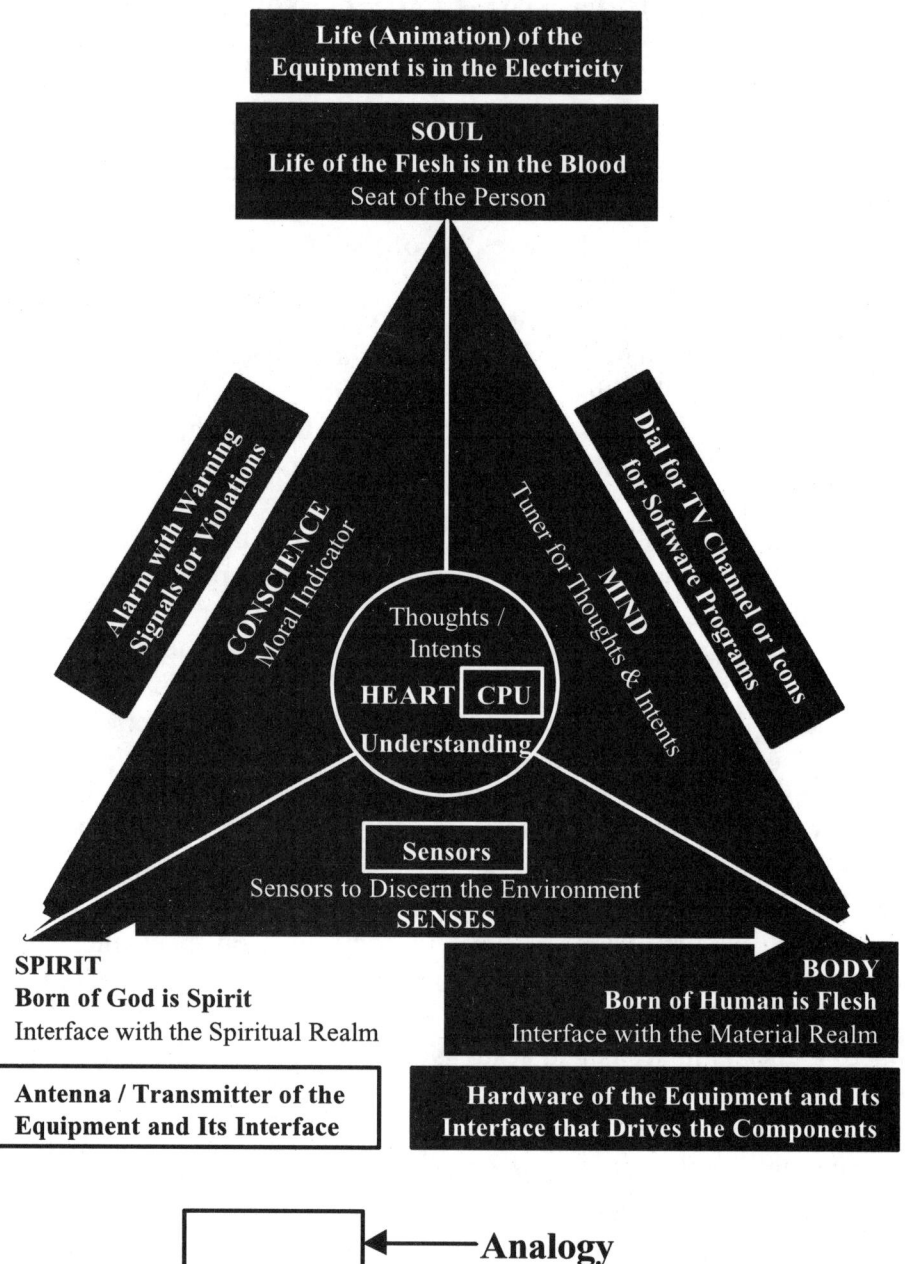

Analogy for the Spirit of Humankind

The operations of our spirit are like unto the functions of the transmitter/antenna in TV transmission. The transmitter installed in a TV station "knows" what is happening inside the station that is apparently hidden to the outsiders. It transmits that information in the form of the light of the knowledge of the glory of images, words and music through the audio-video waves. In this way, the will and emotions of the author/creator of those TV shows are transmitted to people in remote places. At the receiving end, there are TVs tuned and immersed (baptized) into the influence zone of the transmission. The antenna of any of those local TV "sees" and "hears" the information and manifests through a TV set. What is shown as the light of the knowledge of the glory of the images on TV screen and what is spoken and sung by the speakers are not of the TV set but of a remote source.

Similarly, our spirit knows the things inside us that are hidden to others. The spirit could transmit that information to God through prayer and worship in the Holy Spirit. In this way, our will and emotions are communicated to God in heaven. Also, our spirit "sees" and "hears" the things of God and His kingdom through the Holy Spirit. They manifest in our heart in the form of the light of the knowledge of the glory of images, words and music through the Holy Spirit. What are seen and heard as dreams and visions as well as hymns and psalms and spiritual songs in our heart are not of us but of heaven.

The visual summary for the make-up of a human being together with the analogy is reproduced on the page to the left. The bottom left corner of the triangle and the adjacent box are highlighted. The summary description pertaining to our spirit and the corresponding analogy can be found within the highlighted area at the bottom left corner of the triangle and inside the adjacent box, respectively.

Our spirit is the interface for us to interact in the realm of the spirit where God lives and His kingdom exists. Also, the living or dead condition of our life is solely dependent on our saved or lost condition in regard to God. For it is our faith in Jesus that causes us to be born of God and receive a new spirit. We may identify the existence of our spirit in three primary ways with reference to God in heaven, us (self) and others. By our newborn spirit, we gain ability to know God, His kingdom and what's in us. Others discern our spirit through the attitudes that we radiate even in the absence of our speech and deeds.

The Bible reveals that all of us sinned and died, and live under the power of Satan. Our spirit loses the ability to know or communicate with

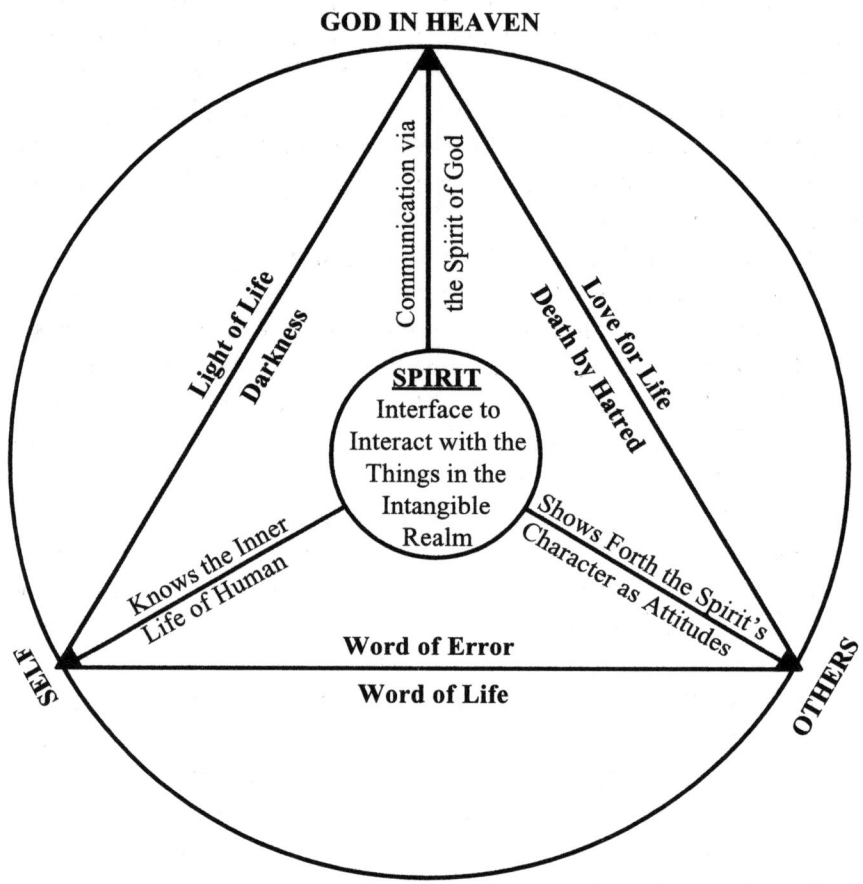

Character and Functions of the Spirit of Humankind

God. Under the dominion of evil, even the light we have in us will be darkness, for we live in the shadow of death. God is the only one who is able to convey us from power of darkness to kingdom of His Son through our faith in Jesus. If we are born again and receive the new spirit, we may be able to see the kingdom of God with the help of the Holy Spirit. We may have the light of life, word of life, love for life in us through our spirit. It empowers us to communicate and have fellowship with the Father, the Son and the Holy Spirit. Since eternal life is to know true God and His Christ, we may abide in eternal life by this ability to know God and see the kingdom of God.

There is a spirit in us and the inspiration of the Almighty gives us understanding. The spirit of a human is the Lamp of the LORD, searching our inmost being. Whenever we morally fail our spirit is troubled, because our spirit discerns the terror of God's judgment and may be overwhelmed at occasions. However, after we repent, our spirit makes a diligent search to find whether we have received the grace and mercy of God during these times of trouble. Therefore, man knows the things of a man except the spirit of the man, which is in him. Despite our circumstances, the spirit of our understanding therefore causes us to face the challenges of life. For example, the spirit will sustain us in sickness.

Now, we consider others discerning our spirit through our attitudes. If we rule our own spirit, we manifest positive spiritual character attributes and eliminate any deceit in our spirit. When we recognize our total dependence on God, we become humble in spirit and retain honor. If we are patient in spirit, we are slow to anger and have great understanding and a calm spirit. If we are of a faithful spirit, we conceal the matter and not reveal secrets. Therefore, the hidden person of the heart, with the incorruptible beauty of a faithful, pure, humble, patient, gentle and quiet spirit, is very precious in the sight of God.

On the contrary, if we do not receive a new spirit, we may manifest forth evil attributes owing to our separation from the goodness of God. Even when all our ways look pure in our own eyes, LORD weighs the spirits. We shouldn't be like those whose spirit is not faithful to God. He that is hasty of spirit easily gets angry and exalts folly. Perverseness in our speech is a breach/flaw in the spirit. A haughty spirit goes before a fall. Lord hates a proud look that stems from a proud spirit. God resists the proud, but gives grace to the humble. Therefore, we who have a proud spirit frustrate the grace of God. Therefore, let us cleanse ourselves from all filthiness of the spirit, perfecting holiness in the fear of God.

A visual summary on page 44 is presented for the character and functions of our spirit. As shown within the center circle of the diagram, our spirit is the interface for us to interact with the things in the intangible realm. We become alive unto God, once we have a new spirit born of God. We can identify the existence and the functions of our spirit in three primary ways. They are summarized along the arrows radiating from the center circle. These ways are in regard to us (self), God in heaven and others as shown around the circle and pointed by the arrows at the corners of the triangle. The condition of our life, when we are alienated from the life of God, is shown along the interior sides of the triangle. On the contrary, we may be united with God and let the fullness of Godhead dwell in us. The condition that results by the life of God in us is shown along the exterior sides of the triangle. For we have newborn spirit and are baptized with the Holy Spirit.

Bible References

The Origin and the Immaterial Nature of the Human Spirit

God Is Our Creator Who Gave Us Our Spirit (Breath): ^{6}By the word of the LORD the heavens were made, and *all the host of them by the breath of His mouth.*$_{(Ps\ 33:6)}$ ^{7}And *the LORD God* formed man of the dust of the ground, and *breathed into his nostrils the breath of life*; and man became a living being.$_{(Gen\ 2:7)}$ ^{4}The Spirit of God has made me, and *the breath of the Almighty gives me life.*$_{(Job\ 33:4)}$ ^{10}In whose hand is the life of every living thing, and *the breath of all mankind*?$_{(Job\ 12:10)}$ ^{14}If He should set His heart on it, *if He should gather to Himself His Spirit and His breath,* ^{15}*All flesh would perish together, and man would return to dust.*$_{(Job\ 34:14-15)}$

People Have No Power over Their Spirit to Retain the Spirit on the Day It Will Return to God Who Gave It: ^{8}*No one has power over the spirit to retain the spirit*, and no one has power in the day of death.$_{(Eccl\ 8:8)}$ ^{3}Do not put your trust in princes, nor in a son of man, in whom there is no help. ^{4}*His spirit departs, he returns to his earth*; in that very day his plans perish.$_{(Ps\ 146:3-4)}$ ^{7}Then the dust will return to the earth as it was, and *the spirit will return to God who gave it.*$_{(Eccl\ 12:7)}$ ^{21}Who knows *the spirit of the sons of men, which goes upward*, and the spirit of the animal, which goes down to the earth?$_{(Eccl\ 3:21)}$

We Can Discern the Existence of Our Immaterial Spirit: ^{37}But they were terrified and frightened, and *supposed they had seen a spirit*. ^{38}And He said to them, "Why are you troubled? And why do doubts arise in your hearts? ^{39}"Behold My hands and My feet, that it is I Myself. Handle Me and see, for *a spirit does not have flesh and bones as you see I have.*" ^{40}When He had said this, He showed them His hands and His feet.$_{(Luke\ 24:37-40)}$ ^{5}Jesus answered, "Most assuredly, I say to you, unless one is born of water and the Spirit, he cannot enter the kingdom of God. ⁶"That which is born of the flesh is flesh, and that *which is born of the Spirit is spirit*. ⁷"Do not marvel that I said to you, 'You must be born again.' ⁸"*The wind blows where it wishes, and you hear the sound of it, but cannot tell where it comes from and where it goes. So is everyone who is born of the Spirit.*"(John 3:5-8) ⁸⁰So *the child grew and became strong in spirit*, and was in the deserts till the day of his manifestation to Israel.(Luke 1:80)

Character Attributes of the Spirit of Humankind

Positive Attributes of Our Spirit: ³²He who is slow to anger is better than the mighty, and *he who rules his spirit* than he who takes a city.(Prov 16:32) ⁸The end of a thing is better than its beginning; *the patient in spirit is better than the proud in spirit*.(Eccl 7:8) ²³A man's pride will bring him low, but *the humble in spirit* will retain honor.(Prov 29:23) ²⁷He who has knowledge spares his words, and a man of understanding is of *a calm spirit*.(Prov 17:27) ¹³A talebearer reveals secrets, but *he who is of a faithful spirit* conceals a matter.(Prov 11:13) ²Blessed is the man to whom the LORD does not impute iniquity, and *in whose spirit there is no deceit*.(Ps 32:2)

Negative Attributes of Our Spirit: ¹⁸Pride goes before destruction, and *a haughty spirit before a fall*. ¹⁹Better to be of *a humble spirit* with the lowly, than to divide the spoil with the proud.(Prov 16:18-19) ⁸And may not be like their fathers, a stubborn and rebellious generation, a generation that did not set its heart aright, and *whose spirit was not faithful to God*.(Ps 78:8) ²⁹He that is slow to wrath is of great understanding: but *he that is hasty of spirit exalteth folly*.(Prov 14:29) ⁹*Do not hasten in your spirit to be angry*, for anger rests in the bosom of fools.(Eccl 7:9) ⁴A wholesome *tongue* is a tree of life: but *perverseness therein is a breach in the spirit*.(Prov 15:4)

Light for the Discernment by the Spirit

We Have the Light for Discernment by Our Spirit to Know About Humankind with the Help of God: ²⁷*The spirit of a man is the lamp of the LORD*, searching all the inner depths of his heart.(Prov 20:27) ⁸But *there is a spirit in man: and the inspiration of the Almighty giveth them understanding*.(Job 32:8KJV) ³I have heard the reproof that reproaches me, and *the spirit of my understanding causes me to answer*.(Job 20:3) ¹¹For *what man knows the things of a man except the spirit of the man which is in him*? Even so no one knows the things of God except the Spirit of God.(1 Cor 2:11) ¹⁶*The Spirit Himself bears witness with our spirit* that we are children of God. ¹⁴For as many as are led by the Spirit of God, these are sons of God. ¹⁵For you did not receive the spirit of bondage again to fear, but *you received the Spirit of adoption by whom we cry out, "Abba, Father.*"(Rom 8:16,14-15) ²Oh, that I were as in months past, as in the days when God watched over me; ³When *His lamp shone upon my head*, and when *by His light* I walked through darkness; ⁴Just as I was in the days of my prime, when the friendly counsel of God was over my tent.(Job 29:2-4)

We Discern God's Judgment by Our Spirit: ³Suffer me that I may speak; and after that I have spoken, mock on. ⁴As for me, is my complaint to man? and if it were so, *why should not my spirit be troubled*?(Job 21:3-4KJV) ²All the ways of a man are pure in his own eyes, but *the LORD weighs the spirits.*(Prov 16:2) ⁴For the arrows of the Almighty are within me; *my spirit drinks in their poison*; the terrors of God are arrayed against me.(Job 6:4) ³I remembered God, and was troubled; I complained, and *my spirit was overwhelmed*. Selah ⁶I call to remembrance my song in the night; I meditate within my heart, *and my spirit makes diligent search*. ⁷Will the Lord cast off forever? And will He be favorable no more? ⁸Has His mercy ceased forever? Has His promise failed forevermore? ⁹Has God forgotten to be gracious? Has He in anger shut up His tender mercies? Selah."(Ps 77:3,6-9)

The Human Spirit at the Death and Resurrection of the Body

The Body Dies When Our Spirit Departs and Gets Resurrected When Our Spirit Comes Back: ²⁶For as *the body without the spirit is dead*, so faith without works is dead also.(James 2:26) ⁵⁹And they stoned Stephen as he was calling on God and saying, *"Lord Jesus, receive my spirit."*(Acts 7:59) ⁴⁶And when Jesus had cried out with a loud voice, He said, *"Father, 'into Your hands I commit My spirit.'"* Having said this, He breathed His last.(Luke 23:46) A little sick girl died before Jesus arrived ⁵⁴But He put them all outside, took her by the hand and called, saying, "Little girl, arise." ⁵⁵*Then her spirit returned, and she arose immediately*. And He commanded that she be given something to eat.(Luke 8:54-55)

A New Spirit for Humankind Through God's New Covenant

We Can Know True God and Have Eternal Life by Becoming a Partaker of the New Covenant: ³¹"Behold, the days are coming, says the LORD, when I will make a new covenant with the house of Israel and with the house of Judah-- ³²"not according to the covenant that I made with their fathers in the day that I took them by the hand to lead them out of the land of Egypt, My covenant which they broke, though I was a husband to them, says the LORD. ³³"But this is the covenant that I will make with the house of Israel after those days, says the LORD: I will put My law in their minds, and write it on their hearts; and I will be their God, and they shall be My people. ³⁴"No more shall every man teach his neighbor, and every man his brother, saying, 'Know the LORD,' for *they all shall know Me*, from the least of them to the greatest of them, says the LORD. For I will forgive their iniquity, and their sin I will remember no more."(Jer 31:31-34) ³"And *this is eternal life, that they may know You*, the only true God, and Jesus Christ whom You have sent.(John 17:3)

God's Promise for a New Spirit for Humankind: ²⁵"Then I will sprinkle clean water on you, and you shall be clean; I will cleanse you from all your filthiness and from all your idols. ²⁶"*I will give you a new heart and put a new spirit within you*; I will take the heart of stone out of your flesh and give you a heart of flesh. ²⁷"I will put My Spirit within you and cause you to walk in My statutes, and you will keep My judgments and do them.(Ezek 36:25-27)

Receiving a New Spirit Through Repentance

God Saves Such as Who Have Contrite Spirit: [13]A merry heart makes a cheerful countenance, but *by sorrow of the heart the spirit is broken.*(Prov 15:13) [22]A merry heart does good, like medicine, but *a broken spirit dries the bones.*(Prov 17:22) [14]The spirit of a man will sustain him in sickness, but *who can bear a broken spirit?*(Prov 18:14) [7]*Answer me speedily, O LORD; my spirit fails*! Do not hide Your face from me, lest I be like those who go down into the pit.(Ps 143:7) [17]*The sacrifices of God are a broken spirit*, a broken and a contrite heart-- these, O God, You will not despise.(Ps 51:17) [3]"*Blessed are the poor in spirit*, for theirs is the kingdom of heaven.(Matt 5:3) [18]*The LORD is near to those who have a broken heart, and saves such as have a contrite spirit.* [19]Many are the afflictions of the righteous, but the LORD delivers him out of them all.(Ps 34:18-19) [10]Create in me a clean heart, O God, and *renew a steadfast spirit within me*. [11]Do not cast me away from Your presence, and do not take Your Holy Spirit from me. [12]Restore to me the joy of Your salvation, and *uphold me by Your generous Spirit.*(Ps 51:10-12)

We Can Receive a New Spirit from God That Enables Us to Follow Him: [30]"Therefore I will judge you, O house of Israel, every one according to his ways," says the Lord GOD. "Repent, and turn from all your transgressions, so that iniquity will not be your ruin. [31]"Cast away from you all the transgressions which you have committed, and *get yourselves a new heart and a new spirit*. For why should you die, O house of Israel? [32]"For I have no pleasure in the death of one who dies," says the Lord GOD. "Therefore turn and live!"(Ezek 18:30-32) [19]"Then I will give them one heart, and *I will put a new spirit within them*, and take the stony heart out of their flesh, and give them a heart of flesh, [20]"that *they may walk in My statutes and keep My judgments and do them*; and they shall be My people, and I will be their God.(Ezek 11:19-20)

Birth of a New Spirit in Humankind Under the New Covenant: [5]Jesus answered, "Most assuredly, I say to you, unless one is born of water and the Spirit, he cannot enter the kingdom of God. [6]"That which is born of the flesh is flesh, and that *which is born of the Spirit is spirit.* [7]"Do not marvel that I said to you, 'You must be born again.' (John 3:5-7) [16]*The Spirit Himself bears witness with our spirit* that we are children of God. [14]For as many as are led by the Spirit of God, these are sons of God. [15]For you did not receive the spirit of bondage again to fear, but *you received the Spirit of adoption by whom we cry out, "Abba, Father."*(Rom 8:16,14-15) [9]Furthermore, we have had human fathers who corrected us, and we paid them respect. Shall we not much more readily be in *subjection to the Father of spirits and live?*(Heb 12:9)

We Are Joined to the Lord in One Spirit with Him: [45]And so it is written, "The first man Adam became a living being." *The last Adam became a life-giving spirit*. [46]However, the spiritual is not first, but the natural, and afterward the spiritual. [47]The first man was of the earth, made of dust; the second Man is the Lord from heaven.(1 Cor 15:45-47) [6]For this reason the gospel was preached also to those who are dead, that they might be judged according to men in the flesh, but *live according to God in the spirit.*(1 Pet 4:6) [16]Or do you not know that he who is joined to a harlot is one body with her? For "the two," He says, "shall become one flesh." [17]But *he who is joined to the Lord is one spirit with Him.*(1 Cor 6:16-17) [12]Thou hast granted me life and favour, and *thy visitation* *hath preserved my spirit.*(Job 10:12KJV) [22]*The Lord Jesus Christ be with your spirit*. Grace be with you. Amen.(2 Tim 4:22) [18]Brethren, *the grace of our Lord Jesus Christ be with your spirit*. Amen.(Gal 6:18)

Nature and Character of a Newborn Spirit

Our Spirit Is Made Perfect in True Righteousness and Holiness: [23]to the general assembly and *church of the firstborn* who are registered in heaven, to God the Judge of all, *to the spirits of just men made perfect.*(Heb 12:23) [23]and *be renewed in the spirit of your mind,* [24]and that you put on the new man which was created according to God, in true righteousness and holiness.(Eph 4:23-24) [6]For to be carnally minded is death, but *to be spiritually minded is life and peace.*(Rom 8:6) [3]Do not let your adornment be merely outward-- arranging the hair, wearing gold, or putting on fine apparel-- [4]rather *let it be the hidden person of the heart, with the incorruptible beauty of a gentle and quiet spirit*, which is very precious in the sight of God.(1 Pet 3:3-4) [7]For God has not given us a *spirit of fear, but of power and of love and of a sound mind.*(2 Tim 1:7)

Darkness to Light: [9]But you are a chosen generation, a royal priesthood, a holy nation, His own special people, that you may proclaim the praises of Him *who called you out of darkness into His marvelous light*;(1 Pet 2:9) [5]*You are all sons of light* and sons of the day. We are not of the night nor of darkness.(1 Thes 5:5) [27]*The spirit of a man is the lamp of the LORD*, searching all the inner depths of his heart.(Prov 20:27) [8]For *you were once darkness, but now you are light in the Lord*. Walk as children of light(Eph 5:8)

New Ability to Discern God and His Kingdom by the Newborn Spirit

Discerning the Things of God and His Kingdom by Our Newborn Spirit: [17]that the God of our Lord Jesus Christ, the Father of glory, *may give to you the spirit of wisdom and revelation in the knowledge of Him,* [18]the eyes of your understanding being enlightened; that you may know what is the hope of His calling, what are the riches of the glory of His inheritance in the saints,(Eph 1:17-18) [13]And since *we have the same spirit of faith*, according to what is written, "I believed and therefore I spoke," we also believe and therefore speak.(2 Cor 4:13) [3]I have heard the reproof that reproaches me, and *the spirit of my understanding causes me to answer.*(Job 20:3) [4]As for me, is my complaint to man? and if it were so, *why should not my spirit be troubled?*(Job 21:4)

Discerning the Spirits in Human (Born Again Spirit verses Unregenerate Spirit): [1]Beloved, do not believe every spirit, but test the spirits, whether they are of God; because many false prophets have gone out into the world. [2]By this you know the Spirit of God: *Every spirit that confesses that Jesus Christ* has come in the flesh is of God, [3]and every spirit that does not confess that Jesus Christ has come in the flesh is not of God. And this is the spirit of the Antichrist, which you have heard was coming, and is now already in the world. [4]You are of God, little children, and have overcome them, because He who is in you is greater than he who is in the world. [5]They are of the world. Therefore they speak as of the world, and the world hears them. [6]*We are of God. He who knows God hears us*; he who is not of God does not hear us. By this *we know the spirit of truth and the spirit of error.*(1 Jn 4:1-6)

Living the Life of God or Evil Through Our Body

Once again, visualizing the scenario when God made first man Adam and first woman Eve may help us to understand the frame and occupants of our body. LORD God formed man of the dust of the ground, and breathed into his nostrils the breath of life; and man became a living soul. Later, LORD God caused a deep sleep to fall upon the man, and he slept; then He took one of his ribs, and closed up the flesh at that place. And the LORD God fashioned into a woman the rib, which He had taken from the man, and brought her to the man. And the man said, "This is now bone of my bones, and flesh of my flesh; she shall be called woman, because she was taken out of Man."

According to God's plan, beginning from Adam and Eve, man and woman become one flesh in sexual union. It is the way humankind multiplies and fills the earth even today. We receive the body from our earthly parents, for what is born of the flesh is flesh. The very original source of our flesh from Adam and Eve explains why we find all basic constituents of our body in the dust of the ground. Also, we ought to feed the body with food and drink that come out of the earth to develop and sustain our physical life. The wages of sin is death. The death therefore entered the world by sin of Adam. It then spread to all humankind, because all have sinned. As a result, all of us are appointed to die once. When we die, our body goes back to earth where it came from.

There is however a day of the resurrection of the dead. The natural body that is sown in corruption, dishonor and weakness will be raised as an incorruptible, glorious and powerful spiritual body. In other words, as we have borne the image of the man (Adam) of dust, we shall also bear the image of the heavenly man (Jesus). If we die in Christ, we will receive a glorious body on the day of resurrection. The body all the others receive will be destroyed with their soul in hell forever.

A number of occupants may dwell in our earthly body. At the minimum, the body houses our spirit and soul. It also has the potential to become the temple of the Holy Spirit. According to the Bible, even the evil spirits possess the bodies of some people. On the contrary, the body can be separated either from the Spirit of God, or evil spirits, or our spirit and soul. If we do not belong to God's family, the body is separated from the Holy Spirit. We can drive out the evil spirits from a demon possessed person by exercising God given authority in Jesus name. Even our spirit and soul depart the body on the day of our death. Therefore, our natural

Gaining Your Ability to Interact with God

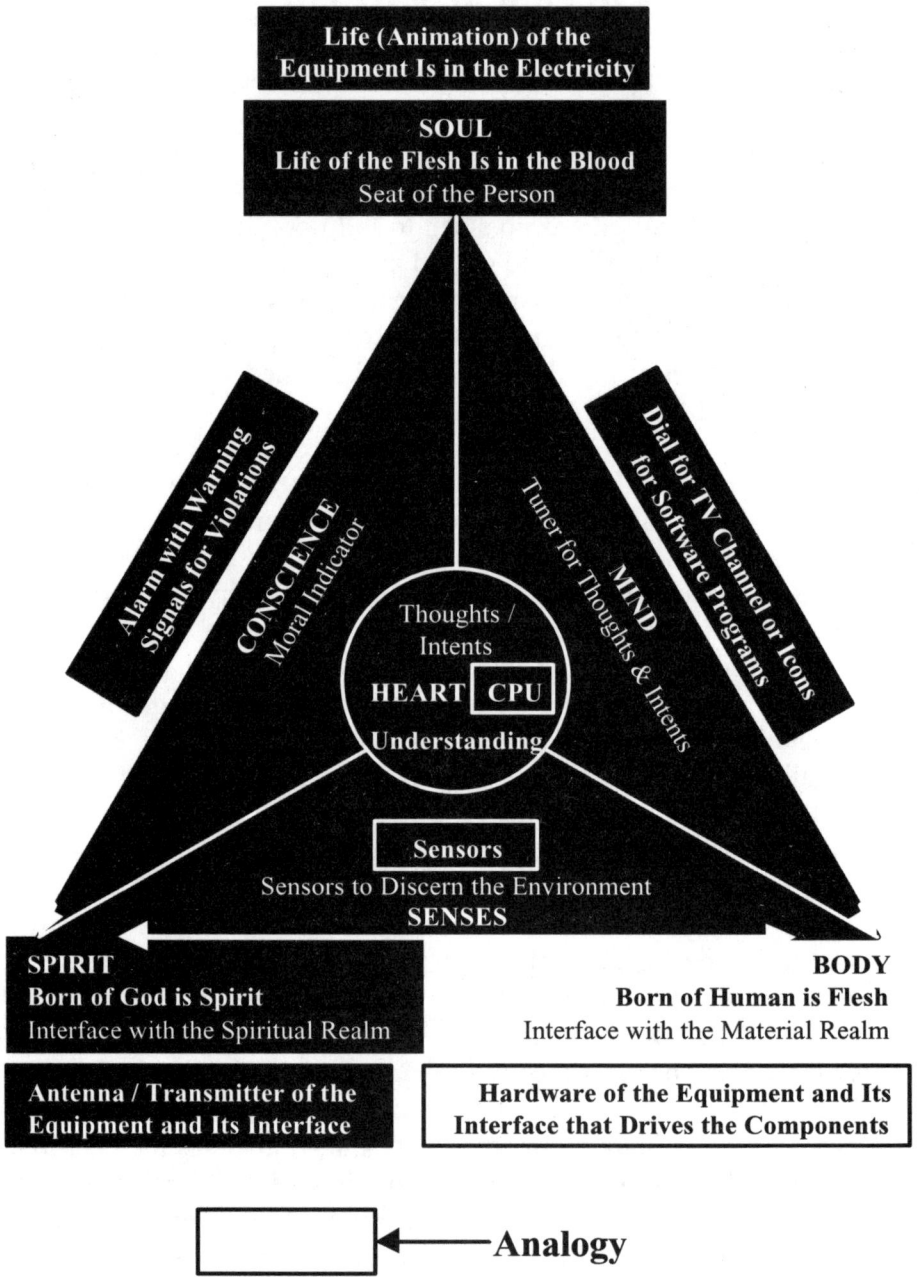

Analogy for the Body of Humankind

and spiritual birth, freewill choices and death determine the occupants of our body.

The make-up of our body can be thought of as the hardware of any electrical or electronic equipment that employs computers. All of the hardware components are made of the things of the earth. Silica chips that form the basic component in computer storage and intelligence are also of the earth. The components such as memory units to store software programs and data, speakers, displays, sensors and physically moving parts generally make up the equipment. The sensors may include cameras for the sight, microphones for the sound, thermometers for the temperature, and pieces that measure humidity, air and water quality etc. We can enhance our understanding about the make-up of our body by comparing these hardware components to the following parts of our body. The components of the equipment, the corresponding parts of the body and the underlying functions are listed below for the purpose of analogy.

Equipment	**Body**	**Function**
Memory Units	Brain	Storage for programs & data
Cameras	Eyes	Sight
Microphones	Ears	Hearing
Moving Parts	Legs & Hands	Physical Work
Speakers	Tongue	Speech
Air Blowers	Lungs	Air to burn the fuel/food
Wiring System	Nervous System	Electrical Signal Transfer
Pumps	Heart	Pressure to Distribute
Water System	Blood System	Distribution by Pressure

The senses are seated in the body just as the sensors are seated in the hardware of the equipment. The nervous system is like the wiring system that collects various signals from the senses (sensors). The heart and the blood distribution system are like the pump and the distribution system for fuel, water and other coolants. The lungs are like air blowers that get the air inside to burn the fuel (food) and also to cool down the heated components inside the equipment. The tongue is like the speakers in the equipment. The hands and legs are like the moving parts of the equipment that do the physical work. Some examples with most of these components may include fully equipped households, cars, trains, planes and rockets.

The visual summary for the make-up of human being together with the analogies is reproduced on page 52. The bottom right corner of the triangle and the adjacent box are highlighted. The summary description for the body and the corresponding analogy can be found within the highlighted area at the bottom right corner of the triangle and inside the adjacent box, respectively.

We who are in the immediate neighborhood can meddle and directly operate the equipment. The people from afar also may operate the equipment through a remote control mechanism if it is connected through unseen waves. The equipment however should have the antenna/transmitter kind of ability to be remote controlled. Similarly, if we are our own lord (flesh), our body could be the vehicle for our will, plan and purposes to manifest in this physical realm. If we however submit to other leaders including God, other people and prince of the air (Satan) our bodies become the vessels to manifest their will, plan and purposes. Since we cannot see God in heaven and Satan with our natural senses we may appear to be remotely controlled.

Our body could house not only our spirit and soul, but also Holy Spirit and evil spirits. In other words, the body could either become the temple of the Holy Spirit or possessed by Satan or evil spirits, often referred as demons. The life (soul) of the flesh is in the blood. Since soul is the seat of our person, the leader to whom our soul would submit controls the animation of our body.

One of the functions of our body is to multiply by giving birth to human babies. The body is also an interface for the inner human to interact with the tangible material world. We acquire information by our senses. We communicate with our mouth the will, plan and purposes and carry them out using our bodily members.

The leaders of our soul include our flesh, god of this world Satan and God of heaven. The will, plan and purposes of our life therefore are going to be determined by our choice for our leader. What information we are going to gather using our senses is also dependent on the leader of our choice. The following paragraphs describe the way we interact with our leaders internally and live our life externally in this earthly body.

If we make us our leader of our soul, we end up walking in the flesh. We who are after the flesh therefore do mind the things of the flesh. The carnal mind is enmity against God and is not subject to the law of God, neither indeed can be. Therefore, carnally minded is death. So then we who are in the flesh cannot please God. For our heart will be filled with thoughts and intents that promote us to lordship at the expense of God and others. The wisdom displayed in this kind of living is sensual, devilish and earthly. The thoughts and intents of our heart that result from a carnal mind are continuously evil and may take control of our speech and deeds. In other words, we manifest forth the will, ways, plan and purposes according to the flesh. The speech of our mouth and deeds of our body may therefore communicate and carry out the will, plan and purposes of our flesh.

Now, we consider making the god of this world the leader of our soul. In this case, we set our mind on the things of the spirit of the world. As a result, our heart will be filled with thoughts and intents pertaining to god of this world. For we yield to Satan (devils/evil spirits) who fills our heart. We search our heart and know the principalities and powers of this dark world. If the body is filled with evil spirit(s) it takes control of our speech and deeds. In other words, we manifest forth the will, ways, plan and purposes according to the spirit of the world. Consequently, the speech of our mouth and deeds of our body will communicate and carry out the will, plan and purposes of god of this world. The lamp of our body is the eye. If our eye is good, our whole body will be full of light. But if our eye is evil, our whole body will be full of darkness. If therefore the light that is in us is darkness, how great is that darkness! No one can serve two masters; for either we will hate the one and love the other, or else we will be loyal to the one and despise the other. We cannot serve God and the spirit of the world at the same time.

On the other hand, we could choose to become new covenant partakers in Christ. As a result, the life activities of our body will show the life of God whenever we submit to Him through the Spirit of God. For our body becomes the vessel in which God dwells and flows as rivers of living water. If we set our mind on the things of the Spirit of God, our heart will be filled with the thoughts and intents pertaining to God. For we yield to the Spirit of God who fills us and pours God's love in our heart.

Now, we consider us making God the leader of our soul through Jesus Christ. In this case, we have a new spirit, new heart and the Holy Spirit within us. We can therefore search our heart and know what the mind of the Spirit is, for He makes intercession according to the will of God. Since the body is the temple of the Holy Spirit we can put to death the deeds of the body by the Holy Spirit. In other words, we can overcome the will, ways, plan and purposes of our flesh as well as the

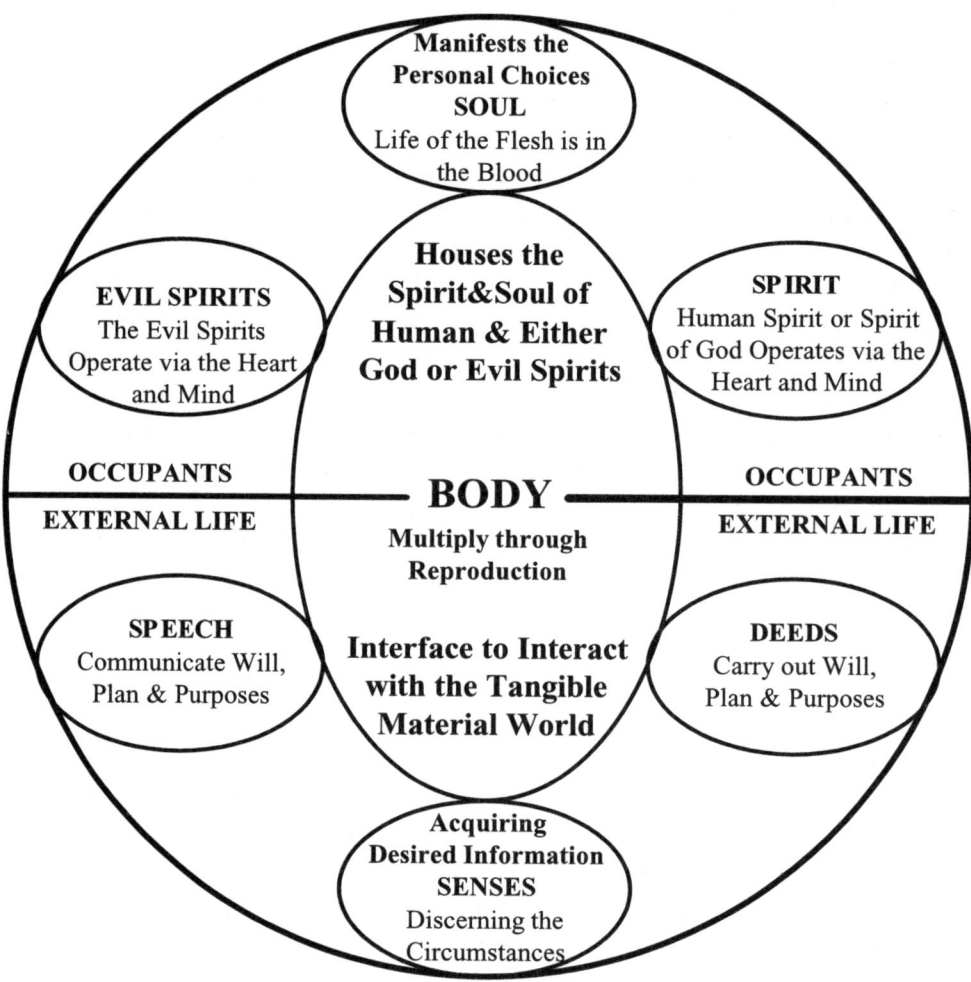

Occupants and Functions of the Human Body

spirit of the world with the help of the Holy Spirit. For the one who is in us is greater than the one who is in the world. Consequently, the speech of our mouth and deeds of our body may communicate and carry out the will, plan and purposes of God. Also, we will be able to rightfully divide the information we acquire through our senses and utilize only that which pertains to God.

A visual summary for the occupants and the functions of our body is shown on the page to the left. As shown within the upper half of the exterior circle, our body could house not only our spirit and soul, but also Holy Spirit and evil spirits. Soul the seat of our person, as shown within the smaller ellipse at the very top, is in the blood. In other words, the life of the flesh is in the blood.

The external manifestation of our life in the body is shown within the bottom half of the exterior circle on left page. As stated within the bottom half of the center ellipse, one of the functions of our body is to multiply in this earth through reproduction. The body is also an interface for the inner person to interact with the tangible material world. As shown within the smaller ellipse at the very bottom, we acquire information by our senses. Also, we communicate with our mouth the will, plan and purposes and carry them out using our bodily members, as shown inside the other two smaller ellipses within the bottom half of the annulus.

The leader to whom our soul will submit controls the animation of our body. Leader of our choice may be those shown inside the ellipses within the top half of the exterior circle. They are either us(flesh), Satan through evil spirits or God through His Spirit. The speech of our mouth and deeds of our body shown within the bottom half of the exterior circle, would therefore communicate and carry out the will, plan and purposes of the leader of our choice. Also, we will filter and utilize only the information acquired by our senses that pertains to the leader of our choice.

Bible References

Body at Death and Resurrection

Body Returns to the Ground at Death of Humankind Due to Sin: ^{7}And ***the LORD God formed man of the dust of the ground***, and breathed into his nostrils the breath of life; and man became a living being.(Gen 2:7) ^{16}And the LORD God commanded the man, saying, "Of every tree of the garden you may freely eat; ^{17}"but of the tree of the knowledge of good and evil you shall not eat, for in ***the day that you eat of it you shall surely die.***"(Gen 2:16-17) [17]Then to Adam He said, "Because you have heeded the voice of your wife, and have eaten from the tree of which I commanded you, saying, 'You shall not eat of it': "Cursed is the ground for your sake; in toil you shall eat of it all the days of your life.(Gen 3:17) [19]In the sweat of your face you shall eat bread till ***you return to the ground, for out of it you were taken; for dust you are, and to dust you shall return.***"(Gen 3:19) [56]***The sting of death is sin.***(1 Cor 15:56) [23]For the wages of sin is death.(Rom 6:23) [12]Therefore, just as through one man sin entered the world, and death through sin, and ***thus death spread to all men***, because all sinned--(Rom 5:12)

We Will Receive a Heavenly Spiritual Body at the Resurrection: [39]All flesh is not the same flesh, but there is one kind of flesh of men, another flesh of beasts, another of fish, and another of birds. [40]There are also celestial bodies and terrestrial bodies; but the glory of the celestial is one, and the glory of the terrestrial is another. [41]There is one glory of the sun, another glory of the moon, and another glory of the stars; for one star differs from another star in glory. [42]So also is the resurrection of the dead. The body is sown in corruption, it is raised in incorruption. [43]It is sown in dishonor, it is raised in glory. It is sown in weakness, it is raised in power. [44]It is sown a natural body, ***it is raised a spiritual body***. There is a natural body, and there is a spiritual body. [45]And so it is written, "The first man Adam became a living being." The last Adam became a life-giving spirit. [46]However, the spiritual is not first, but the natural, and afterward the spiritual. [47]The first man was of the earth, made of dust; the second Man is the Lord from heaven. [48]***As was the man of dust, so also are those who are made of dust; and as is the heavenly Man, so also are those who are heavenly***. [49]And as we have borne the image of the man of dust, we shall also bear the image of the heavenly Man. [50]Now this I say, brethren, that flesh and blood cannot inherit the kingdom of God; nor does corruption inherit incorruption.(1 Cor 15:39-50)

Resurrected Bodies Will Not Go Through Sexual Experience: [33]"***Therefore, in the resurrection, whose wife does she become***? For all seven had her as wife." [34]And Jesus answered and said to them, "The sons of this age marry and are given in marriage. [35]"But ***those who are counted worthy to attain that age, and the resurrection from the dead, neither marry nor are given in marriage***; [36]"***nor can they die anymore, for they are equal to the angels and are sons of God, being <u>sons of the resurrection</u>***. [37]"Now even Moses showed in the burning bush passage ***that the dead are raised***, when he called the Lord 'the God of Abraham, the God of Isaac, and the God of Jacob.'(Luke 20:33-37)

The Body Obtained During Rapture: [51]Behold, I tell you a mystery: We shall not all sleep, but we shall all be changed-- [52]in a moment, in the twinkling of an eye, at the last trumpet. For the trumpet will sound, and ***the dead will be raised incorruptible***, and we shall be changed. [53]For ***this corruptible must put on incorruption, and this mortal must put on immortality***. [54]So when this corruptible has put on incorruption, and this mortal has put on immortality, then shall be brought to pass the saying that is written: "***Death is swallowed up in victory***." (1 Cor 15:51-54)

Living the Life of God by Our Body Through a Life in the Spirit

Jesus Is Our Resurrection and Life Through His Own Flesh and Blood: ²⁵Jesus said to her, "*I am the resurrection and the life*. He who believes in Me, though he may die, he shall live.²⁶"And whoever lives and believes in Me shall never die."(John 11:25-26) ⁵⁴"*Whoever eats My flesh and drinks My blood has eternal life, and I will raise him up at the last day*. ⁵⁶"He who eats My flesh and drinks My blood abides in Me, and I in him. ⁵⁷"As the living Father sent Me, and *I live because of the Father, so he who feeds on Me will live because of Me*."(John 6:54,56,57) ⁷For there are three that bear witness in heaven: the Father, the Word, and the Holy Spirit; and these three are one.⁸And *there are three that bear witness on earth: the Spirit, the water, and the blood*; and these three agree as one.(I Jn 5:7-8)

Jesus Is the Way for God to Enter Through His Spirit and Resurrect Our Bodies Unto Life: ³⁷Jesus stood and cried out, saying, "If anyone thirsts, let him come to Me and drink. ³⁸"He who believes in Me, as the Scripture has said, out of his heart (belly) will flow rivers of living water." ³⁹But this He spoke concerning the Spirit, whom those believing in Him would receive.(John 7:37-39) ²⁶"But the Helper, *the Holy Spirit, whom the Father will send in My name*.(John 14:26) He said ⁶³"*It is the Spirit who gives life*; the flesh profits nothing.(John 6:63) ²For the law of the Spirit of life in Christ Jesus has made me free from the law of sin and death.(Rom 8:2) ¹⁰And if Christ is in you, the body is dead because of sin, but the Spirit is life because of righteousness. ¹¹But if the Spirit of Him who raised Jesus from the dead dwells in you, *He who raised Christ from the dead will also give life to your mortal bodies through His Spirit who dwells in you*. (Rom 8:10-11)

We Can Choose to Be Filled and Sanctified by the Holy Spirit: ¹³"how much more will your heavenly Father give the Holy Spirit to those who ask Him!"(Luke 11:13) Therefore ¹⁸be filled with the Spirit. (Heb 13:18) ²⁵If we live in the Spirit, let us also walk in the Spirit. ¹⁶I say then: Walk in the Spirit, and you shall not fulfill the lust of the flesh. (Gal 5:25,16) ¹⁹Or do you not know that your body is the temple of the Holy Spirit who is in you, whom you have from God, and you are not your own?(1 Cor 6:19) ¹⁷If anyone defiles the temple of God, God will destroy him. For the temple of God is holy, which temple you are. (1 Cor 3:17) ⁹You, however, are controlled not by the sinful nature but by the Spirit, if the Spirit of God lives in you.(Rom 8:9 NIV) ¹⁶that the offering of the Gentiles might be acceptable, sanctified by the Holy Spirit.(Rom 15:16) Therefore ¹³*if by the Spirit you put to death the deeds of the body, you will live*.(Rom 8:13) For ⁸*he who sows to the Spirit will of the Spirit reap everlasting life*.(Gal 6:8)

Life to the Mortal Body by Abiding in the Holy Spirit: ¹⁰If Christ is in you, the body is dead because of sin, but the *Spirit is life* because of righteousness. ¹¹But if the Spirit of Him who raised Jesus from the dead dwells in you, He who raised Christ from the dead will also *give life to your mortal bodies through His Spirit* who dwells in you.(Rom 8:10-11) Jesus said ³⁸He that believeth on me, as the scripture hath said, out of his belly shall *flow rivers of living water*. ³⁹(*But this spake he of the Spirit*, which they that believe on him should receive: for the Holy Ghost was not yet given; because that Jesus was not yet glorified.)(John 7:38-39 KJV) ²²But now having been set free from sin, and having become slaves of God, *you have your fruit to holiness, and the end, everlasting life.*(Rom 6:22)

Deliverance From Bondage to Lawless Deeds, Sickness, Demons and Death by the Entrance of the Spirit (God) in Jesus Name: [2]elect according to the foreknowledge of God the Father, *in sanctification of the Spirit.* (1 Pet 1:2) [38]"Repent, and let every one of you *be baptized in the name of Jesus Christ for the remission of sins; and you shall receive the gift of the Holy Spirit.*(Acts 2:38) Jesus said [26]"But the Helper, the *Holy Spirit, whom the Father will send in My name*, He will teach you all things.(John 14:26) [13]For if you live according to the flesh you will die; but if *by the Spirit you put to death the deeds of the body*, you will live.(Rom 8:13) [10]if Christ is in you, the body is dead because of sin, but the Spirit is life because of righteousness. [11]But if *the Spirit of Him who raised Jesus from the dead dwells in you, He who raised Christ from the dead will also give life to your mortal bodies through His Spirit who dwells in you.*(Rom 8:10-11) Jesus said [28]"But if *I cast out demons by the Spirit of God*, surely the kingdom of God has come upon you.(Matt 12:28) God(Spirit) at His will distribute to us [9]gifts of healings by the same Spirit.(1 Cor 12:9)

Life by God's Grace

God's Grace for All Needs Destroys the Yoke of Bondage to Sin (Lawless Deeds), Sickness, Demons and Death: [8]God is able to make all grace abound toward you, that you, always having all sufficiency in all things, may have an abundance for every good work. [10]Now may He who supplies seed to the sower, and bread for food, supply and multiply the seed you have sown and increase the fruits of your righteousness.(2 Cor 9:8,10) [31]"Therefore do not worry, saying, 'What shall we eat?' or 'What shall we drink?' or 'What shall we wear?' [32]"For after all these things the Gentiles seek. For your heavenly Father knows that you need all these things. [33]"But seek first the kingdom of God and His righteousness, and all these things shall be added to you.(Matt 6:31-33) Because [19]my God shall supply all your need according to His riches in glory by Christ Jesus.(Phil 4:19)

Grace Might Reign Through Holiness and Resurrection to Eternal Life: [14]*Pursue peace with all people, and holiness, without which no one will see the Lord:* [15]*looking diligently lest anyone fall short of the grace of God.*(Heb 12:14-15) [14]For sin shall not have dominion over you, for you are not under law but under grace. [22]But *now having been set free from sin, and having become slaves of God, you have your fruit to holiness, and the end, everlasting life.* [23]For the wages of sin is death, but the gift of God is eternal life in Christ Jesus our Lord. (Rom 6:14,22-23) and also [14]knowing that *He who raised up the Lord Jesus will also raise us up with Jesus*, and will present us with you. [15]For all things are for your sakes, *that grace, having spread through the many, may cause thanksgiving to abound to the glory of God.*(2 Cor 4:14-15)

Living the Life of Evil by the Body by a Life Driven by the Flesh

We Who Refuse to Have Faith in Jesus Christ Remain Natural and Cannot Know the Holy Spirit: Jesus said [26]"But the Helper, the *Holy Spirit, whom the Father will send in My name.*(John 14:26) [17]"the Spirit of truth, whom the world cannot receive, *because it neither sees Him nor knows Him.*(John 14:17) [63]"It is the Spirit who gives life; the flesh profits nothing.(John 6:63) Therefore [14]the natural man does not receive the things of the Spirit of God, for they are foolishness to him; nor can he know them, because they are spiritually discerned.(1 Cor 2:14)

No Entry of God for Those of Us Who Are Carnal and Will Not Love God in Jesus: [3]For this is the love of God, that we keep His commandments.(1 Jn 5:3) [22]Judas (not Iscariot) said to Him, "Lord, how is it that *You will manifest Yourself to us, and not to the world*?"[23]Jesus answered and said to him, "If anyone loves Me, he will keep My word; and My Father will love him, and We will come to him and make Our home with him. [24]"*He who does not love Me does not keep My words.*(John 14:22-24) [9]Now *if anyone does not have the Spirit of Christ, he is not His*.(Rom 8:9) [5]For those who live according to the flesh set their minds on the things of the flesh.(Rom 8:5)[6]For to be carnally minded is death.(Rom 8:6) [7]Because the carnal mind is enmity against God; for it is not subject to the law of God, nor indeed can be. [8]So then, those who are in the flesh cannot please God.(Rom 8:7-8) [8]For he who sows to his flesh will of the flesh reap corruption.(Gal 6:8) [13]For if you live according to the flesh you will die.(Rom 8:13) [5]Therefore He who supplies the Spirit to you and works miracles among you, does He do it by the works of the law, or by the hearing of faith?--(Gal 3:5) Indeed [14]*we might receive the promise of the Spirit through faith*.(Gal 3:14)

We Cannot Sanctify Our Deeds and Live Without the Help of the Holy Spirit:[19]Now the works of the flesh are evident, which are: adultery, fornication, uncleanness, lewdness, [20]idolatry, sorcery, hatred, contentions, jealousies, outbursts of wrath, selfish ambitions, dissensions, heresies,[21]envy, murders, drunkenness, revelries, and the like; of which I tell you beforehand, just as I also told you in time past, that those who practice such things will not inherit the kingdom of God. (Gal 5:19-21) [17]The kingdom of God is not eating and drinking, but righteousness and peace and joy in the Holy Spirit.(Rom 14:17) [5]For *when we were in the flesh, the sinful passions which were aroused by the law were at work in our members to bear fruit to death*. [6]But now we have been delivered from the law, having died to what we were held by, so that we should serve in *the newness of the Spirit* and not in the oldness of the letter.(Rom 7:5-6) [17]For *the flesh lusts against the Spirit, and the Spirit against the flesh*; and these are contrary to one another, so that you do not do the things that you wish. [16]I say then: Walk in the Spirit, and you shall not fulfill the lust of the flesh.(Gal 5:17,16)

Evil Life by the Body Controlled by the Spirit of the World

Evil Spirits Works in the Sons of Disobedience: [1]And you He made alive, who were dead in trespasses and sins,[2]in which *you once walked according to the course of this world, according to the prince of the power of the air, the spirit who now works in the sons of disobedience*, [3]among whom also we all once conducted ourselves in the lusts of our flesh, fulfilling the desires of the flesh and of the mind, and were by nature children of wrath, just as the others.(Eph 2:1-3)

People May Follow Doctrines of Demons and Become Insensitive to Things of God: [1]Now the Spirit expressly says that in latter times some will depart from the faith, *giving* heed to deceiving spirits and doctrines of demons,²speaking lies in hypocrisy, having their own conscience seared with a hot iron(1 Tim 4:1-2)

Many Evil Spirits Can Indwell a Person and Control His Life: ²⁷And when He stepped out on the land, there met Him a certain man from the city who had demons for a long time. And he wore no clothes, nor did he live in a house but in the tombs. ²⁸When he saw Jesus, he cried out, fell down before Him, and with a loud voice said, "What have I to do with You, Jesus, Son of the Most High God? I beg You, do not torment me!" *²⁹For He had commanded the unclean spirit to come out of the man. For it had often seized him, and he was kept under guard, bound with chains and shackles; and he broke the bonds and was driven by the demon into the wilderness. ³⁰Jesus asked him, saying, "What is your name?" And he said, "Legion," because many demons had entered him.* ³¹And they begged Him that He would not command them to go out into the abyss. ³²Now a herd of many swine was feeding there on the mountain. And they begged Him that He would permit them to enter them. And He permitted them. ³³Then the demons went out of the man and entered the swine, and the herd ran violently down the steep place into the lake and drowned.(Luke 8:27-33)

People Can be Repossessed by More Unclean Spirits: Jesus said ²³"He who is not with Me is against Me, and he who does not gather with Me scatters. ²⁴"When an unclean spirit goes out of a man, he goes through dry places, seeking rest; and finding none, he says, 'I will return to my house from which I came.' ²⁵"And when he comes, he finds it swept and put in order. ²⁶"*Then he goes and takes with him seven other spirits more wicked than himself, and they enter and dwell there; and the last state of that man is worse than the first.*"(Luke 11:23-26)

Casting Out Evil Spirits

Casting Demons by the Spirit of God: ²⁴Now when the Pharisees heard it they said, "This fellow does not cast out demons except by Beelzebub, the ruler of the demons." ²⁵But Jesus knew their thoughts, and said to them: "Every kingdom divided against itself is brought to desolation, and every city or house divided against itself will not stand. ²⁶"If Satan casts out Satan, he is divided against himself. How then will his kingdom stand? ²⁷"And if I cast out demons by Beelzebub, by whom do your sons cast them out? Therefore they shall be your judges. ²⁸"But if *I cast out demons by the Spirit of God*, surely the kingdom of God has come upon you.(Matt 12:24-28) ²⁰"But *if I cast out demons with the finger of God, surely the kingdom of God has come upon you.*(Luke 11:20)

We Can Cast out the Evil Spirits in the Name of Jesus: Jesus said ¹⁷"And these signs will follow those who believe: *In My name they will cast out demons*; they will speak with new tongues;(Mark 16:17) ¹⁶Now it happened, as we went to prayer, that a certain slave girl possessed with a spirit of divination met us, who brought her masters much profit by fortune-telling. ¹⁷This girl followed Paul and us, and cried out, saying, "These men are the servants of the Most High God, who proclaim to us the way of salvation." ¹⁸And this she did for many days. But Paul, greatly annoyed, turned and said to the spirit, "*I command you in the name of Jesus Christ to come out of her." And he came out that very hour.*(Acts 16:16-18)

Natural and Spiritual Discernment by Our Senses

The senses of our body help us to live a quality physical life. We need air, food, and suitable weather conditions to sustain our life in this body. We may get sick or even die, if we are separated from either air or food for certain period of time. The death may also occur due to exposure to extreme hot or cold weather conditions. The senses for taste, smell and feeling indeed help us to monitor: a healthy food plan; an environment with clean air; and an exposure to suitable weather conditions, respectively. Moreover, we need light and sound to see and hear with our eyes and ears. The senses for sight and hearing help us to communicate and understand our natural environment in which our life in the flesh is seated. Separation from light and sound can cause accidents and death as it handicaps our movements involved in our daily activities. We therefore, save, provide, protect and restore our life in the flesh with the help of our senses.

The spiritual senses, on the other hand, help us to live an abundant eternal life. We need the breath of God, spiritual food, and suitable spiritual conditions to sustain our life in the spirit. We abide in spiritually dead condition, when we are separated from the presence of God. It includes the breath of the almighty, the light of God, the word of God, the Spirit of God and the love of God. When we abide in death, we may continuously be influenced or oppressed or possessed by evil spirits due to absence of indwelling God's presence.

When we are born of God however, we receive a new spirit, new heart and the Holy Spirit within us. As a result, we will have the light of life, word of life, spirit of life and love for life residing in us. We will be able to live a life in the spirit within the kingdom of God using our spiritual senses as described below.

Similar to tasting food and drink for the well being of our physical life, we taste the word of God and drink Jesus blood and the Spirit for the well being of our eternal life. We see the natural things of the world in sunlight. Similarly, we see in our heart the glory of God and the things of God's kingdom in God's light. It may include seeing visions and dreams by the Spirit of God. We hear words, noises and music from the animate and the inanimate things in our natural environment. Similarly, we hear words, hymns and psalms and spiritual songs in our heart pertaining to God and His kingdom. Sight and hearing help us to communicate and understand our spiritual environment in which our life in the spirit is

Gaining Your Ability to Interact with God

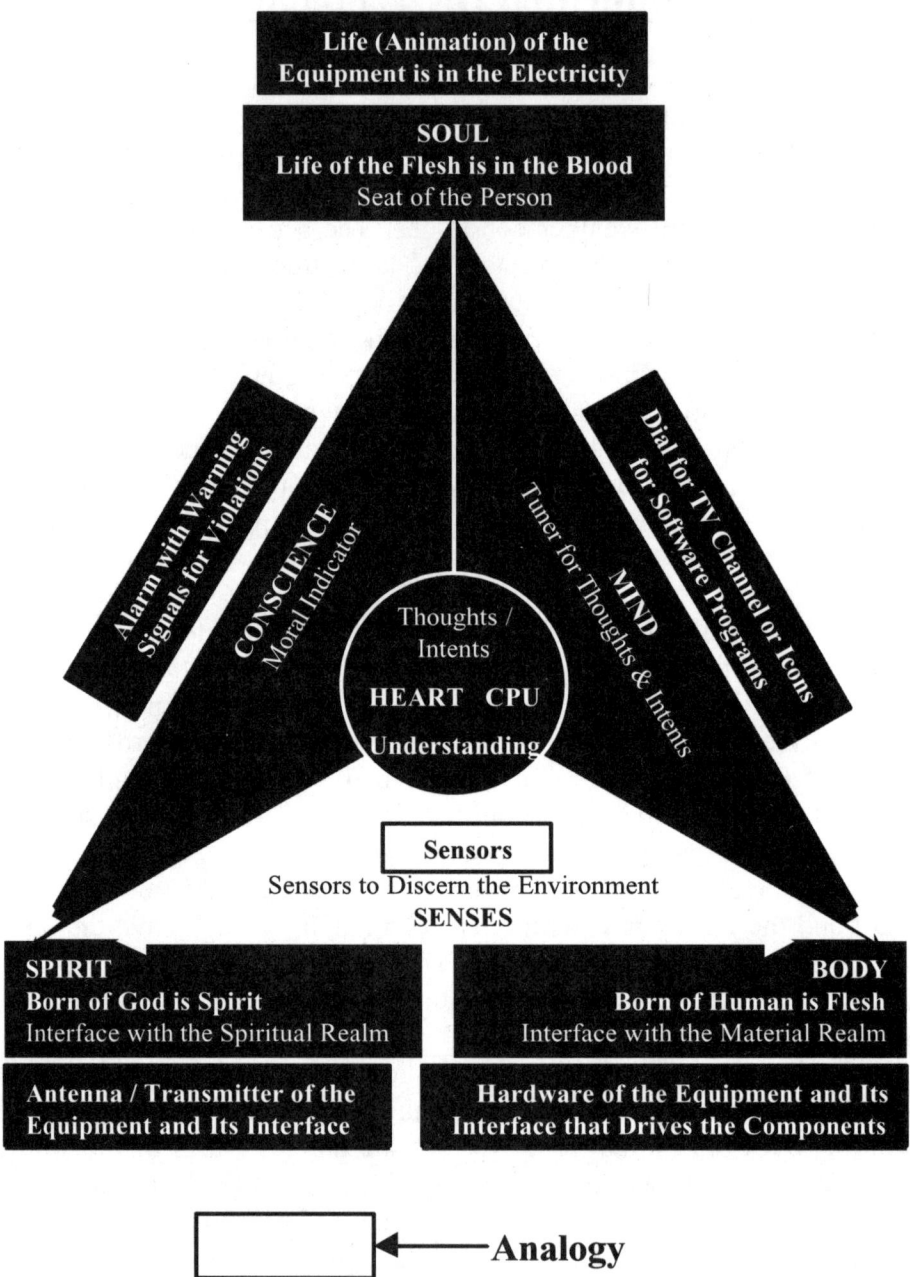

Analogy for the Senses of Humankind

seated. Staying away from light and voice of God may be harmful and prone to cause accidents. Similar to our touch with air, people and things in the natural realm, we touch the things of God in the spiritual realm. For the spirit of God comes upon us and lives in and through us. We breathe air to sustain our life in the flesh. Similarly, the breath of God sustains our breath of the spirit of life. We therefore, save, provide, protect and restore our life in the spirit by the help of our spiritual senses.

The visual summary for the make-up of a human being together with the analogy is reproduced on the page to the left. The bottom triangular sector within the exterior triangle is highlighted. As shown inside the highlighted area, the senses help us to discern the environment. The senses are compared to sensors in equipment as shown within the box adjacent to senses. The discernment by senses extends to life in the flesh as well as the life in the spirit, as indicated by the arrows along the bottom side of the triangle. A comprehensive comparison of senses in regard to the life in the flesh and the life in the spirit is tabulated below.

Senses	**Life in the Flesh**	**Life in the Spirit**
Taste	Natural food & drinks	Jesus flesh, blood & the Spirit of God
Touch	Air, people & things	God's Spirit and things of His Kingdom
Smell	Breathing the air	Breath of the Almighty
Sight	Seeing in sunlight	Seeing in God's light
Hearing	Words and sounds	Words and sounds from spiritual realm

Various ingredients used in our food and drinks are usually identified by their taste. The discernment of the taste warns us to avoid items that are harmful to our body. When we eat food, the sensors in our mouth enable us to understand the corresponding taste in our heart. It certainly helps us to enjoy various food and drink items. Simultaneously, we come to know the suitability of those things that we feed into our body to sustain our life in the flesh. Even if we accidentally swallow poisonous items the identification by taste causes us to take timely remedial measures to restore our health condition.

The sense for taste could be compared to sensors used for quality monitoring in food industry. A CPU, like our heart, loaded with relevant software programs identifies the food ingredients when it receives the signals from sensors. It warns us of any undesirable components including various harmful preservatives and food ingredients. It even makes recommendations about the acceptability of food item as it is or with proposed remedial measures. The consumer representatives from regulatory agencies accept or reject those items based on those findings and recommendations.

Sense for taste in the realm of the spirit is similar in many ways to the one in the material realm. We sustain the life in the spirit by feeding on the flesh and blood of Jesus and the Spirit of God. Jesus said that He was the bread came down from heaven, that we might eat of it and not die. Whoever eats Jesus flesh and drinks His blood therefore has eternal life. Since Jesus was the very embodiment of the word of God, feeding on the word sustains our life. When we taste the word, we will come to know in our heart whether they are of God or Satan. Feeding on the principalities of darkness is harmful to our life in the spirit. If we happen to swallow the principalities from the spirit of the world, we can cleanse ourselves by the blood of Christ in repentance and be safe.

The odors of various gases and solids are different. We gain understanding of the smell of a substance in our heart by breathing into our nostrils the air that surrounds it. It helps us to enjoy smelling flowers as well as the aroma of various food items. We also come to know whether the air that sustains our life in the flesh is desirable to breathe in. For the discernment of the smell warns us of undesirable places and substances we encounter in our daily life. It aids us to avoid or to take remedial measures to improve the air pollution in our environment.

The sense for smell could be compared to sensors used for air quality monitoring in environmental engineering. A CPU, like our heart, loaded with relevant software programs identifies the contents of the air when it receives the signals from sensors. It warns us of any harmful substances beyond admissible limits present in the air. It even makes proposals about the remedial measures to improve air quality. The department of motor vehicles uses a smog test to regulate the air quality based on those kind of findings.

The breath of the Almighty gives us life in the spirit, just as the breathing of air sustains our life in the flesh. Indeed, God gives the breath and the spirit for all of us who walk on the face of the earth. As far as the breath of God is in our nostrils we have the breath of the spirit of life. If God should gather to Himself His Spirit and His breath all flesh would perish together and we would return to dust. This is similar to individuals who drown in water and die due to separation from the air.

We feel differently when we are exposed to different climatic conditions. These may include hot and humid summers, dry and cold winters, comfortable springs and colorful autumns. Also, we discern the warm feelings of love and concern when we come in contact with others. This can be in the form of shaking hands or kissing or hugging or even sexual activities between spouses. Contrarily, we also discern the wounding feelings when others physically discipline or abuse us. Those people may include our family members, schoolteachers, criminals and government authorities. We gain understanding of those feelings in our heart whenever our skin touches the air or people or other tangible things around us. It helps us to enjoy our environment as well as to avoid any detrimental conditions in our circumstance.

The sense for feeling by touch is similar to receiving signals from sensor for humidity, thermometer for temperature and barometer for pressure. Also, the presence of wounding hurricanes or earthquakes may be discerned by the signals received from sensor for wind speed and seismometer for ground acceleration etc. A CPU, like our heart, loaded with relevant software programs identifies the measurements for desired parameters from the signals from sensors. It warns us of any harmful circumstances when measured parameters exceed certain limits. It even makes recommendations for preparedness to protect us from any significant damages from anticipated crises. The weatherman makes his daily news essentially based on similar findings and recommendations.

Similar to our sense for feeling by the physical touch we have our spiritual sense for touch in the realm of the spirit. One of the examples for physical touches includes male and female becoming one flesh in a sexual union. Similarly, one who is joined to the Lord is one spirit with Him. For we are the temple of God and the spirit of the Father, the spirit of the Son and the Holy Spirit dwell in us. Also, the Holy Spirit pours the love of God in our heart. Jesus who is the intercessor for this union said to His disciples that I in you and you in me and I in the Father and Father in me to explain this spiritual union. Even we are advised in the Bible to continue to be filled with the Holy Spirit. All of these show a spiritual sense of touch with God to know our spiritual atmosphere at any time.

The light from those things where our eyes are focused is going to enter into our body through the lenses of our eyes. That in turn shines forth the light of the knowledge of the glory of those images in our heart. This can be compared to a TV camera that receives the light through its lenses from those objects on which it is focused. And the LCD display shines forth the light of the knowledge of the glory of those images. If we choose to focus our eyes on ungodly things even the light we have in our

Gaining Your Ability to Interact with God

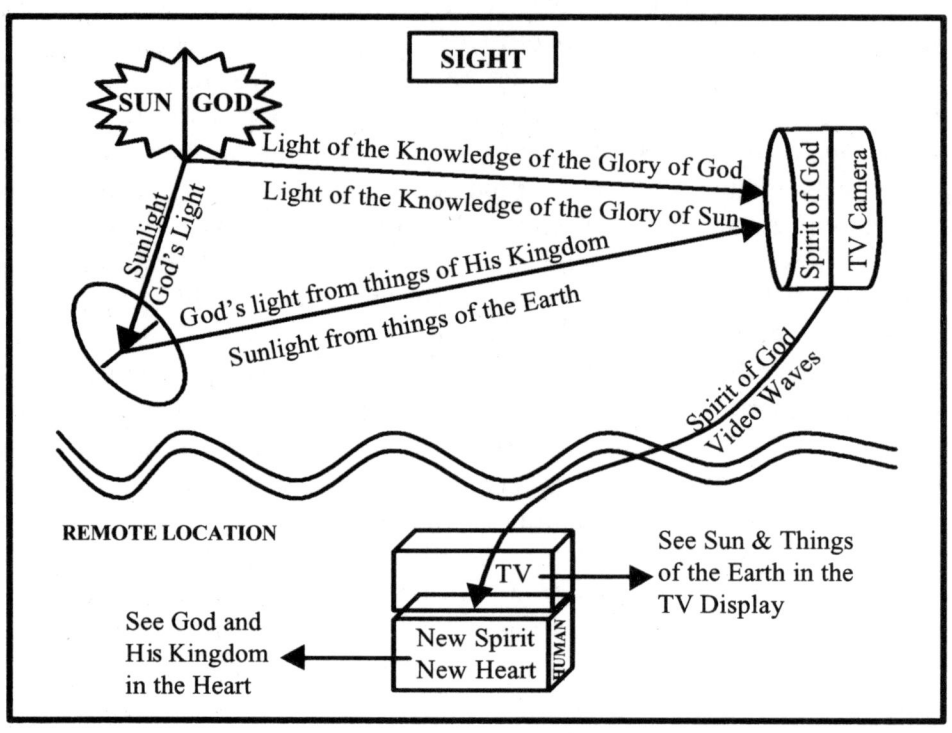

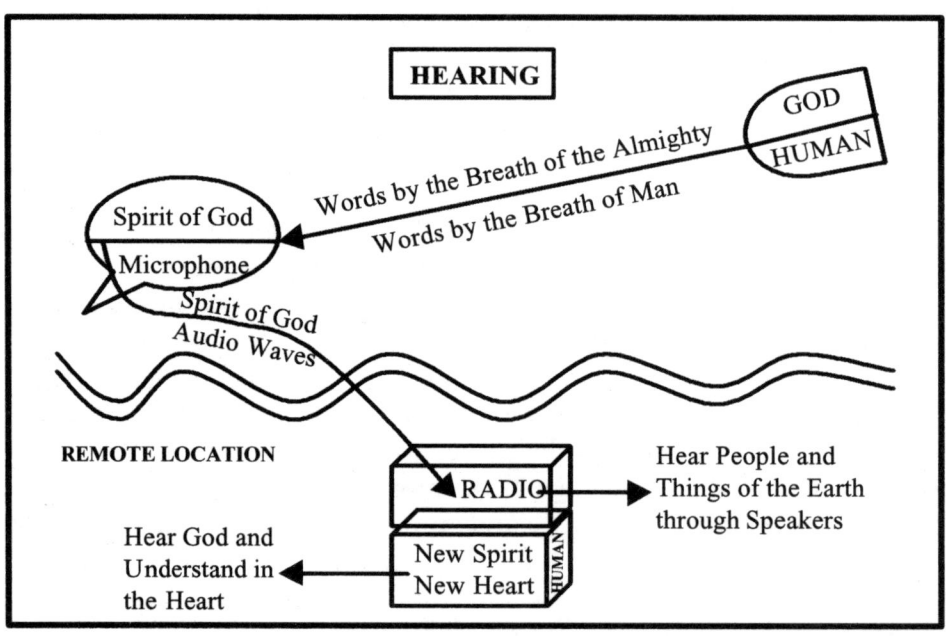

body will be darkness. On the contrary, if we direct our focus on godly things our body will be full of light, having no part of darkness. Now we consider the illustrative diagram within the top rectangular frame on the page to the left to contrast between the spiritual and natural senses for the sight. We know that God is light and in His light we see light. As shown within the star at the top left corner, the sources of spiritual and natural light are God and sun, respectively.

The natural light, as illustrated within the top rectangular frame on left page, could be received into the TV camera located closer to the right edge in two different ways. They are, as shown by the arrows, the light directly from the sun and the sunlight from an object after reflection. These rays cause the light of the knowledge of the glory of the sun and the earthly things to be received within the TV camera. The knowledge of images, as illustrated at the bottom half of the frame, could be carried by video-waves and displayed by a TV located at a remote place.

Consider the remaining texts on the same arrows and inside the objects within the top rectangular frame on left page. They illustrate the comparison between the natural and the spiritual realm. The Spirit of God is shown next to the TV camera in the natural realm. For He receives the light of the knowledge of the glory of God and the light from the things of God's Kingdom in the realm of the spirit. The Spirit also, as shown at the bottom half of the top frame, carries that information like the video waves in the natural realm and reveals it to our heart. He sometimes shows them in the form of dreams and visions similar to a TV display. If we follow Jesus, we will have the light of life in us. For the eternal life in Jesus is the light for us to see the light of the knowledge of the glory of God and His kingdom. In other words, once we are born again, the new heart, new spirit and the Holy Spirit within us enable us to see God and His Kingdom in our heart.

When people speak, the sound waves are going to be formed by the compression of the air caused by the breath of their mouth. If we receive that breath into our ears, our heart gains understanding for what is said. In other words, the entrance of the word brings the light for discernment. This is similar to a CPU discerning the sound signals that are received by a microphone. Now we consider the illustrative diagram inside the bottom rectangular frame on left page to contrast between the spiritual and natural senses for hearing. We know that there is a spirit in human beings and the breath of the Almighty gives them understanding. As shown at the top half of the rectangular bottom frame, the breath of the

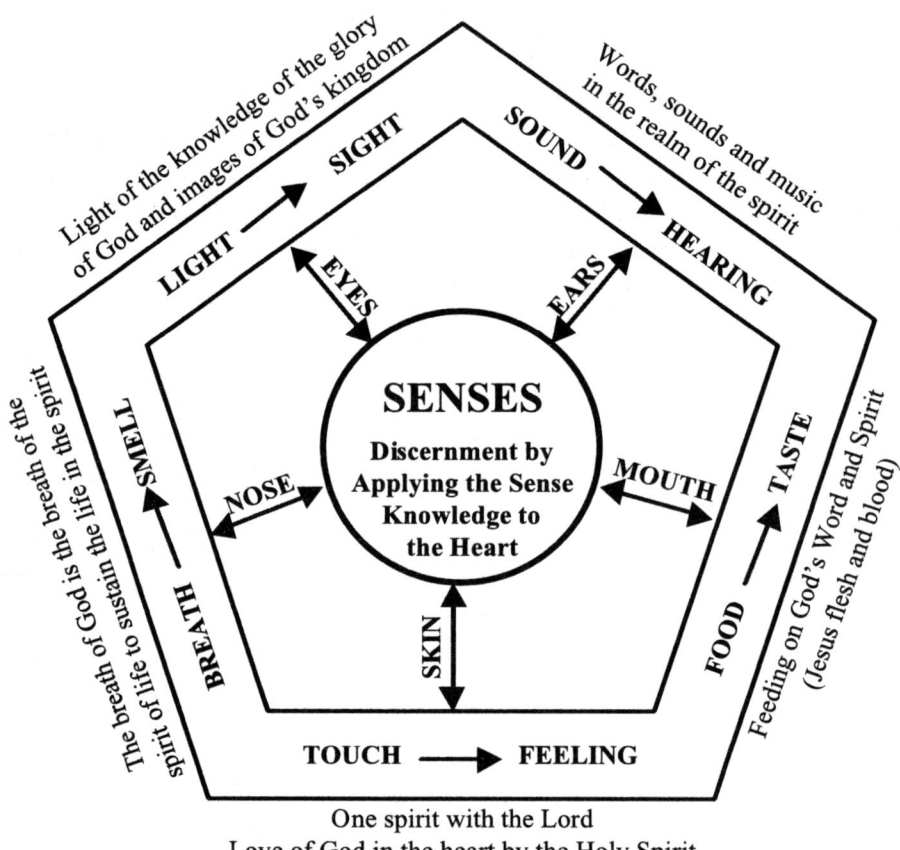

Human Senses for Discernment

Natural and Spiritual Discernment by Our Senses

Almighty and breath of human could form and transmit the words in the spiritual and natural realms, respectively.

In the natural, as illustrated within the top half of the bottom rectangular frame on page 68, the breath of the mouth could be received into a microphone located closer to the left edge of the frame. This enables the words, sounds and music to be carried by audio-waves and broadcast, as shown within the same frame, by a radio located at a remote place.

Consider the remaining texts on the same arrow and inside the objects side by side within the bottom rectangular frame on page 68. They contrast the speaking, transmitting and hearing the words, sounds and music between the natural and the spiritual realm. The Spirit of God is shown next to the microphone in the natural realm. For He receives the word from God in the realm of the spirit. The Spirit also, as shown within the same frame on page 68, carries that information like the audio waves in the natural realm and tells us in our heart. If we follow Jesus, we will know His voice. For the eternal life in Jesus is to know true God and His Christ. In other words, once we are born again, the new heart, the new spirit and the Holy Spirit within us enable us to hear God.

A visual summary for our senses is shown on the page to the left. The five senses are sight, hearing, taste, feeling and smell. They are seated in our bodily members such as eyes, ears, mouth, skin and nose, respectively. These members are shown along the arrows in between the circle and the pentagon. As listed along the pentagon annulus on left page, we see in the light, hear the sound, taste the food, feel the touch and smell by our breath. When we apply the sense knowledge to the heart, as shown within the center circle, we gain understanding. The life in the flesh therefore is made possible by the discernment by our natural senses.

When we receive a new spirit, new heart and the Holy Spirit by our faith in Jesus, we start discerning God and the things of God's kingdom. The life in the spirit by our spiritual discernment is shown outside and along the exterior sides of the pentagon on left page. Once we are born again, we see the light of the knowledge of the glory of God and images of God's kingdom in our heart. We hear words, sounds and music from the realm of the spirit. We taste the Lord as we feed on God's word, Jesus blood and God's spirit for our eternal life. We touch God when He becomes one spirit with us and pour His love in our heart by His Spirit. The breath of God is our breath of the spirit of life that sustains our life in the spirit.

Bible References

Inability of Humankind to Know God by the Natural Senses

Parables Were Used to Explain the Spiritual Things to Be Understood by the Natural Senses: [2]Now Moses called all Israel and said to them: "You have seen all that the LORD did before your eyes in the land of Egypt, to Pharaoh and to all his servants and to all his land-- [3]"the great trials which your eyes have seen, the signs, and those great wonders. [4]"*Yet the LORD has not given you a heart to perceive and eyes to see and ears to hear, to this very day.*(Deut 29:2-4) Jesus then said[13]"Therefore I speak to them in parables, because *seeing they do not see, and hearing they do not hear, nor do they understand*. [14]"And in them the prophecy of Isaiah is fulfilled, which says: 'Hearing you will hear and shall not understand, and seeing you will see and not perceive; [15]For the hearts of this people have grown dull. Their ears are hard of hearing, and their eyes they have closed, lest they should see with their eyes and hear with their ears, lest they should understand with their hearts and turn, so that I should heal them.'(Matt 13:13-15)

We May Not Know the Things of God If We Solely Discern by Our Flesh and Blood (Natural Senses): [16]Simon Peter answered and said, "You are the Christ, the Son of the living God." [17]Jesus answered and said to him, "Blessed are you, Simon Bar-Jonah, for *flesh and blood has not revealed this to you*, but My Father who is in heaven.(Matt 16:16-17) [14]But the *natural man* does not receive the things of the Spirit of God, for they are foolishness to him; *nor can he know them*, because they are spiritually discerned.(1 Cor 2:14) [50]Now this I say, brethren, that *flesh and blood cannot inherit the kingdom of God*; nor does corruption inherit incorruption.(1 Cor 15:50)

Eternal Life by Knowing God by Spiritual Senses and God's Spirit

We Receive a New Spirit, a New Heart and the Holy Spirit for Eternal Life: [26]"*I will give you a new heart and put a new spirit within you*; I will take the heart of stone out of your flesh and give you a heart of flesh. [27]"*I will put My Spirit within you* and cause you to walk in My statutes, and you will keep My judgments and do them.(Ezek 36:26-27) [34]"No more shall every man teach his neighbor, and every man his brother, saying, *'Know the LORD,' for they all shall know Me*, from the least of them to the greatest of them, says the LORD. For I will forgive their iniquity, and their sin I will remember no more."(Jer 31:34) [3]"And *this is eternal life, that they may know You, the only true God, and Jesus Christ* whom You have sent.(John 17:3)

Discernment by Our Spirit with the Help of God: [27]*The spirit of a man is the lamp of the LORD*, searching all the inner depths of his heart.(Prov 20:27) [8]But *there is a spirit in man: and the inspiration of the Almighty giveth them understanding*.(Job 32:8KJV) [3]I have heard the reproof that reproaches me, and *the spirit of my understanding causes me to answer*.(Job 20:3) [11]For *what man knows the things of a man except the spirit of the man which is in him*? Even so no one knows the things of God except the Spirit of God.(1 Cor 2:11) [16]*The Spirit Himself bears witness with our spirit* that we are children of God.(Rom 8:16)

Sight: Eternal Life by Seeing God and His Kingdom in God's Light

God Is Light and in His Light We See Light: [5]This is the message which we have heard from Him and declare to you, that *God is light* and in Him is no darkness at all.(I Jn 1:5) [19]the *LORD will be to you an everlasting light*, and your God your glory.(Isa 60:19) [6]There are many who say, "Who will show us any good?" *LORD, lift up the light of Your countenance upon us.*(Ps 4:6) [15]*In the light of the king's face is life*, and his favor is like a cloud of the latter rain.(Prov 16:15) [9]For *with You is the fountain of life; in Your light we see light.*(Ps 36:9) [1]*The LORD is my light* and my salvation; whom shall I fear? The LORD is the strength of my life; of whom shall I be afraid?(Ps 27:1)

The Life in Jesus Is the Light for Us to See God and His Kingdom: [3]Jesus answered and said to him, "Most assuredly, I say to you, unless one is *born again, he cannot see the kingdom of God*."(John 3:3) [12]Then Jesus spoke to them again, saying, "I am the light of the world. He who follows Me shall not walk in darkness, but *have the light of life*."(John 8:12) [4]In Him was life, and the *life was the light of men.*(John 1:4) Jesus[3] who *being the brightness of His glory and the express image of His person*, and upholding all things by the word of His power, when He had by Himself purged our sins, sat down at the right hand of the Majesty on high,(Heb 1:3) [6]For it is the God who commanded light to shine out of darkness, who has shone in our hearts *to give the light of the knowledge of the glory of God in the face of Jesus Christ.*(2 Cor 4:6)

The Spirit Revealing the Heavenly Things to Us Through Visions and Dreams: [17]'And it shall come to pass in the last days, says God, that I will pour out of My Spirit on all flesh; your sons and your daughters shall prophesy, *your young men shall see visions, your old men shall dream dreams*.[18]And on My menservants and on My maidservants I will pour out My Spirit in those days; and they shall prophesy.(Acts 2:17-18)

Hearing: Eternal Life by Hearing God's Word

We Pass From Death Into Life by Hearing the Word of God: [8]But *there is a spirit in man, and the breath of the Almighty gives him understanding.*(Job 32:8) [24]"Most assuredly, I say to you, *he who hears My word and believes in Him who sent Me has everlasting life,* and shall not come into judgment, but has passed from death into life. [25]"Most assuredly, I say to you, the hour is coming, and now is, when *the dead will hear the voice of the Son of God; and those who hear will live*.(John 5:24-25) [17]"*He who has an ear, let him hear what the Spirit says to the churches*. To him who overcomes I will give some of the hidden manna to eat.(Rev 2:17)

Taste: Eternal Life by Feeding on Jesus Flesh & Blood and the Spirit

Eternal Life by Eating Jesus Flesh and Drinking Jesus Blood: [50]"This is the bread which comes down from heaven, that one may eat of it and not die. [51]"I am the living bread which came down from heaven. If anyone eats of this bread, he will live forever; and the bread that I shall give is My flesh, *which I shall give for the life of the world.*"(John 6:50-51) [53]Then Jesus said to them, "Most assuredly, I say to you, unless you eat the flesh of the Son of Man and drink His blood, you have no life in you.

⁵⁴"*Whoever eats My flesh and drinks My blood has eternal life*, and I will raise him up at the last day. ⁵⁵"For My flesh is food indeed, and My blood is drink indeed.(John 6:53-55) ⁵⁶"He who eats My flesh and drinks My blood abides in Me, and I in him. ⁵⁷"As the living Father sent Me, and *I live because of the Father, so he who feeds on Me will live because of Me.*(John 6:56-57) ⁴For it is impossible for those who were once enlightened, and *have tasted the heavenly gift, and have become partakers of the Holy Spirit,* ⁵*and have tasted the good word of God* and the powers of the age to come, ⁶if they fall away, to renew them again to repentance, since they crucify again for themselves the Son of God, and put Him to an open shame.(Heb 6:4-6)

Drinking of the Spirit of God Who Gives Eternal Life: ¹³For *by one Spirit we were all baptized into one body*-- whether Jews or Greeks, whether slaves or free-- and *have all been made to drink into one Spirit*.(1 Cor 12:13) ¹⁸And do not be drunk with wine, in which is dissipation; but *be filled with the Spirit,*(Eph 5:18) ⁸For he who sows to his flesh will of the flesh reap corruption, but *he who sows to the Spirit will of the Spirit reap everlasting life.*(Gal 6:8) ⁶³"*It is the Spirit who gives life*; the flesh profits nothing. The words that I speak to you are spirit, and they are life.(John 6:63)

Touch: Eternal Life by Being One Spirit with the Lord

We Who Are Joined to the Lord Are One Spirit with Him: ¹⁸For through Him *we both have access by one Spirit to the Father.*(Eph 2:18) ¹⁶Do you not know that you are the temple of God and that *the Spirit of God dwells in you*?(1 Cor 3:16) ⁶And because you are sons, *God has sent forth the Spirit of His Son into your hearts*, crying out, "Abba, Father!"(Gal 4:6) ²⁰"for it is not you who speak*, but the Spirit of your Father who speaks in you.*(Matt 10:20) ¹⁶Or do you not know that he who is joined to a harlot is one body with her? For "the two," He says, "shall become one flesh." ¹⁷But *he who is joined to the Lord is one spirit with Him.*(1 Cor 6:16-17) Jesus said ¹⁹"A little while longer and the world will see Me no more, but you will see Me. *Because I live, you will live also.* ²⁰"*At that day you will know that I am in My Father, and you in Me, and I in you*. (John 14:19-20) ²⁸"*for in Him we live and move and have our being.*'(Acts 17:28)

Smell: Eternal Life by the Breath of the Almighty

Breath of the Spirit of Life for Human by God the Almighty: ⁷And the LORD God formed man of the dust of the ground, and *breathed into his nostrils the breath of life*; and man became a living being.(Gen 2:7) ³As long as my breath is in me, and *the breath of God in my nostrils,*(Job 27:3) ⁴The Spirit of God has made me, and *the breath of the Almighty gives me life.*(Job 33:4) ⁵Thus says God the LORD, who created the heavens and stretched them out, who spread forth the earth and that which comes from it, *who gives breath to the people on it, and spirit to those who walk on it:*(Isa 42:5) ¹⁴If He should set His heart on it, *if He should gather to Himself His Spirit and His breath,* ¹⁵ *All flesh would perish together*, and man would return to dust.(Job 34:14-15) ²¹And all flesh died that moved on the earth: birds and cattle and beasts and every creeping thing that creeps on the earth, and every *man*. ²²*All in whose nostrils was the breath of the spirit of life*, all that was on the dry land, died.(Gen 7:21-22)

Saving of the Soul the Seat of Our Person

The soul is the seat of our person. It interacts with the material world through our life in the flesh and spiritual world through our life in the spirit. The body goes back to the earth on the day of our death. It decays and becomes part of the earth and loses its identity as an individual. Similarly, on the day of our death our spirit goes back to God who gave it. The soul, on the other hand, with our consciousness as a person either goes to heaven or hell. The freewill choices and emotions stem from our proactive and reactive response ability therefore are associated with our soul. The heart, mind and conscience become the processing and implementation center for those responses. We execute those choices and express our emotions through our life in the flesh and the life in the spirit.

Now we consider our life in the flesh. Blood is the life of all flesh, its blood sustains its life. When the blood is flowing through our members, every member functions according to the designed purpose of God. For example, the eyes see, ears hear, the mouth speaks, heart pumps the blood, the lungs breathe the air, nervous system picks up the signals, the brain discerns and stores information and so on. The life that results from the blood flowing through our members of the body is the soul that resides in our body. When people die the soul departs the body and either goes to heaven or hell. The soul however comes back into the body, if God indeed resurrects it. We need not fear those who kill the body but cannot kill the soul. We however should fear God who is able to destroy both soul and body in hell, in case our sin is not atoned for in Jesus. Hell is like unto the prison in a country. The government authorities use it to separate and hold the lawless from the rest of the citizens. Similarly, God separates the lawless from Him and the citizens of His kingdom and puts them in hell.

Our soul may be thought of as the characteristic of any electrical or electronic equipment that exhibits itself, when it becomes "alive" and works. Moreover, the blood to the body may be likened unto the electricity to any electric or electronic equipment. The equipment acts dead as far as the electricity is not passing through its members. On the other hand, the equipment is made alive, once the switch is turned on and the electricity begins to flow through its members. The life of the equipment that shapes its image is in the electricity. For it empowers the equipment to function and manifest forth the life according to its design. For example, a camera sees, microphone hears, sensors pick up the

Gaining Your Ability to Interact with God

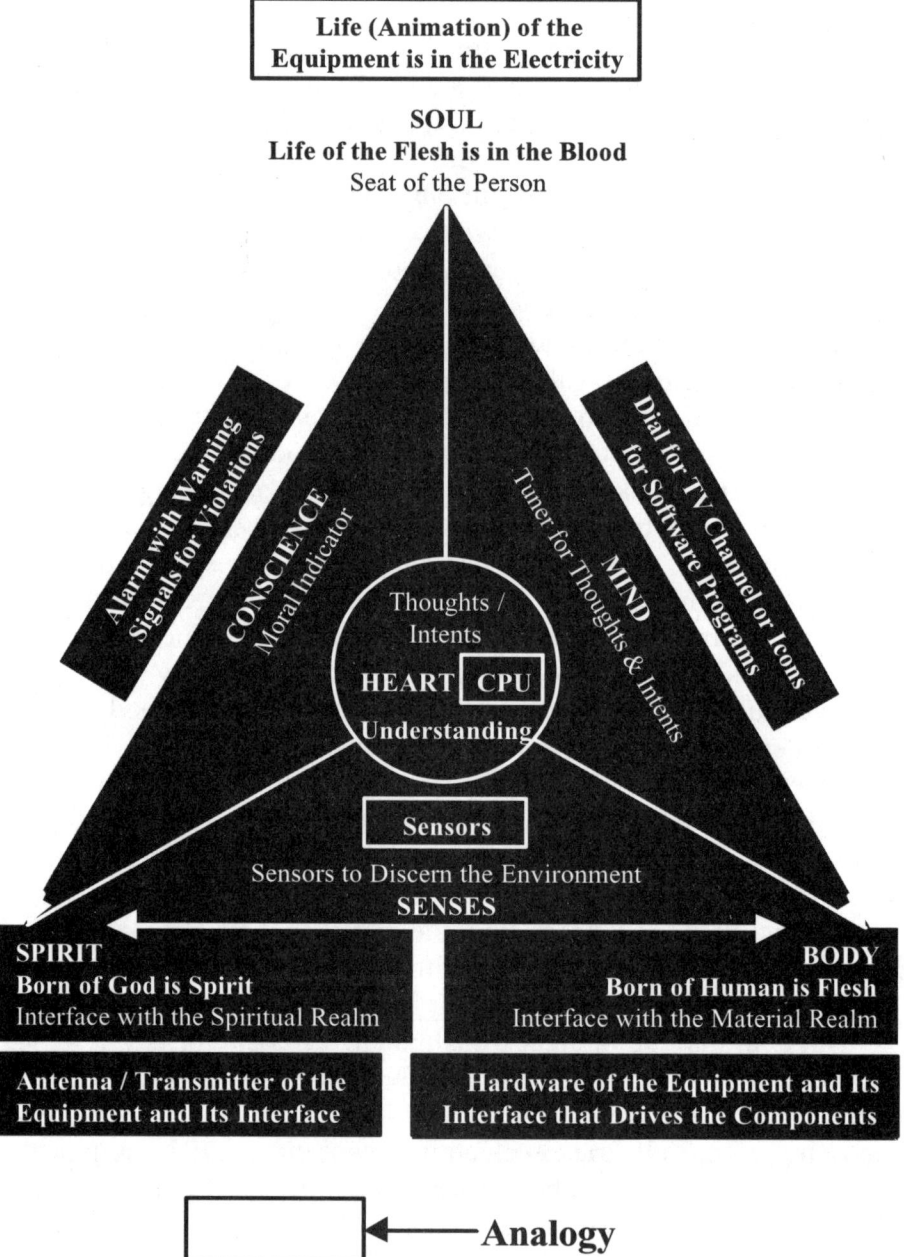

Analogy for the Human Soul

temperature, humidity, air and water quality etc. The hardware and the life of the equipment that is in the electricity can be compared with our body and soul that is in the blood, respectively.

The visual summary for the make-up of human being together with the analogy is reproduced on the page to the left. The top corner of the triangle and the adjacent box pertaining to our soul are highlighted. The summary description for the soul and the corresponding analogy can be found within the highlighted area at the top corner of the triangle and inside the adjacent box, respectively.

When our life is confined to the bodily members, we cannot know God. For the natural human does not discern the things of the Spirit of God for they are spiritually discerned. The flesh and blood therefore cannot inherit the kingdom of God. For we naturally get motivated to speak and do things caring for the things not of heaven but of the earth. In other words, self-promotion (pride), covetousness (lust), passion for the things of this world (idols) and opinion of the world (fear for other people) will be common place in our life. The knowledge and wisdom that result from this kind of life are earthly and devilish. For we readily yield to the principalities, powers, rulers of the darkness of this world and spiritual wickedness in heavenly realm. These are contrary to God's principles, powers, rulers in the kingdom of God that are rooted in righteousness and holiness. Consequently, we may become the vessels for God's wrath. In this kind of lifestyle, even the light we have in us will be darkness. We may be living in an eternally lost condition as far as God and His kingdom are concerned.

Now, we consider the example of flying in a plane to a desired destination. We may visualize a scenario in which the antenna and transmitter in the plane are malfunctioning. The pilot now cannot process the signals from remote sources such as satellites and airports to globally position the flight. This status places the plane in a lost condition with respect to location and destination. In other words, though the essential parts of the plane that make it to fly (soul) are functioning properly the plane is lost. Similarly, if we have a human spirit that cannot discern the light of the knowledge of the glory of the images and words from God and His kingdom, our soul lives in a lost condition. The soul cannot be saved unless otherwise we get a new spirit and a new heart with laws of God written in it. These are similar to the plane inheriting a new antenna/transmitter and a CPU with new programs loaded in it. These new components resurrect the ability to discern the incoming signals.

Gaining Your Ability to Interact with God

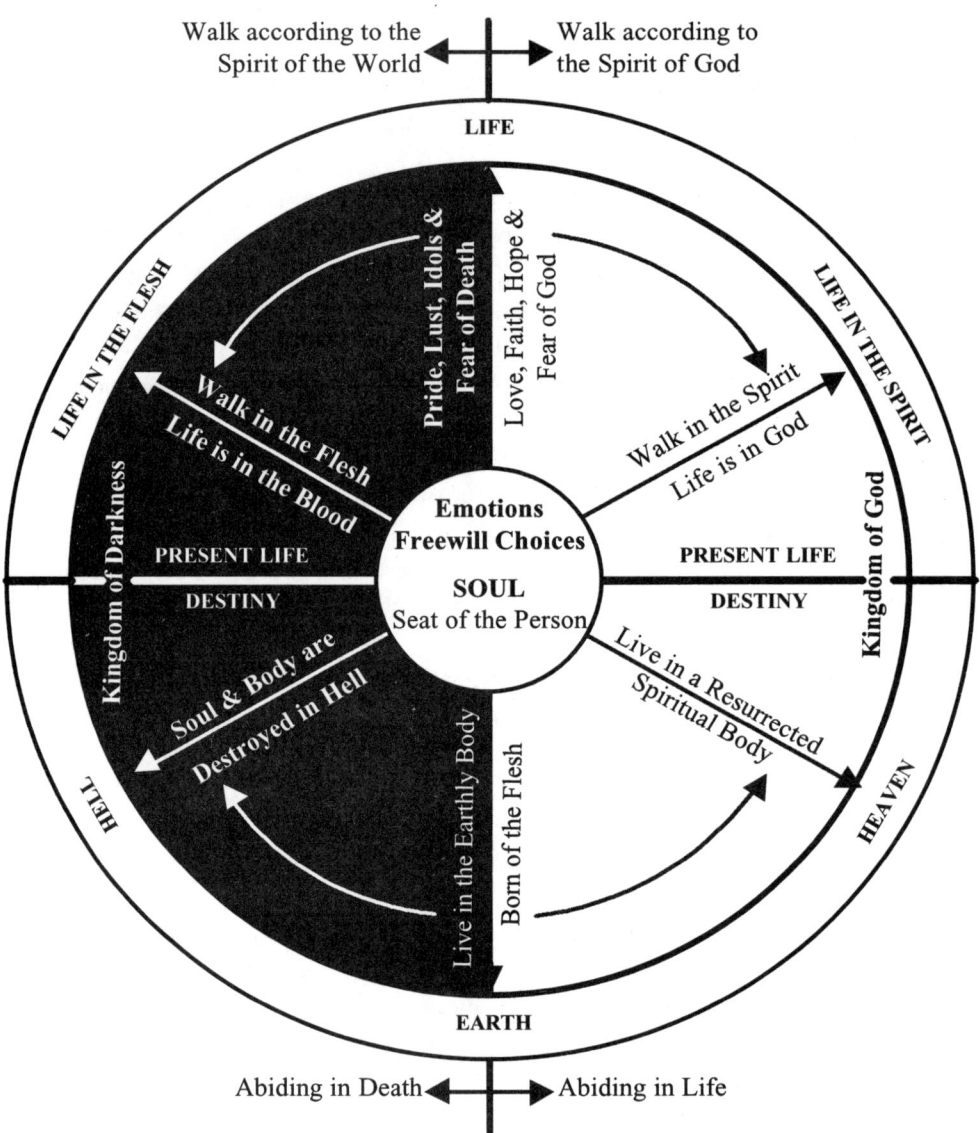

Living Conditions of the Human Soul

God promised us through the prophets to give us a new spirit and a new heart and also to put His Spirit within us to know Him. Moreover, He will write his laws in our heart and minds for us to keep His judgments. When we are born again of God by faith in Jesus, our new man is created after God in righteousness and holiness. We indeed gain the ability to stand right with God and His creation and be separated unto Him.

If we are new covenant partakers in Christ, our body becomes the temple of God. Jesus being the intercessor, the spirit of the Father, the spirit of the Son and the Holy Spirit will dwell in us. Consequently, the eternal life will flow out of our interaction with God. This is similar to a marriage covenant that places the husband and wife under the same roof of a house. And, the married life flows out of the interaction between the husband and wife. We who partake in the new covenant therefore are able to walk in the spirit and live a life for God. For we may walk in the light as God is in the light and see the kingdom of God. If we abide in Jesus, His words and the Holy Spirit, we will live, move and have our being in God. For we will put on the new man and yield to the indwelling God. In essence, if we believe in Jesus, out of our inner man shall flow rivers of living water by the Spirit of God. Detail version of this life in God is found in the book entitled "How to Let God Flow Through you."

On the contrary, if we walk according to the spirit of the world, pride, lust, idols and fear of death will motivate us. As a result, we will walk in darkness and even stumble over the things of God and the people we love. On the other hand, if we are born of the Spirit, life in the spirit is in God. For we have a newborn spirit and a new heart that enable us to walk in the spirit and see the kingdom of God. If we therefore walk according to the Spirit of God, love, faith, hope and fear of God will motivate us. As a result, life in the spirit enables us to walk in the light and live, move and have our being in God.

If we are citizens of the kingdom of God, we will be with God in heaven for eternity. And we will live in a spiritual body from heaven since the day of the resurrection for those who died in Christ. Contrarily, if we dwell in the kingdom of darkness on the day of our death, we will go to hell. And we will live in a body that will be given on the day of the resurrection for those who died without Christ. According to God's judgment, every soul that sins shall surely die. If there is no sin atonement (Christ) in our life therefore, God will destroy our soul and body in hell for eternity.

A visual summary is presented on page 78 for the life of our soul, for a span that extends beyond our present life in this world. The soul, as shown within the center circle, is the seat of our person. The freewill choices and emotions that pertain to our proactive and reactive responses, therefore, stem from our soul. We can freely choose to walk, as shown at the very top of the diagram on page 78, either according to the spirit of God or the spirit of the world. As a result, we live in a condition either described within the right half or the left half of the visual summary. The right half summarizes the life in the kingdom of God. And, the left half summarizes the life in the kingdom of darkness. We, based on our choices therefore, as shown at the very bottom of the diagram on page 78, either abide in a living condition or dead condition in regard to God.

The upper half of the diagram on page 78 shows the present life pertaining to the two kingdoms. As shown by the upward arrow, the motivating factors for our choices in this life are going to be different for both kingdoms. Life in the flesh, as shown within the upper left quadrant, is in the blood. We may not know God by walking in the flesh, for flesh and blood cannot inherit the kingdom of God. Life in the spirit, as shown within the upper right quadrant, is in God. We may see the kingdom of God by walking in the spirit and know God.

The bottom half of the diagram on page 78 shows the destiny of our soul pertaining to the two kingdoms. The destinations including hell and heaven are summarized within the bottom left and right quadrants, respectively. As shown by the arrow directly downward, we now live on the earth in a natural body born of the flesh. On the day of our death, depending on our living or dead condition with regard to God, we will end up in heaven or hell. We will have resurrected bodies either to live in heaven or to be destroyed in hell.

Bible References

The Soul of Humankind and Its Life in the Flesh

Our Life (Animal Soul) Is in the Blood: [11]'For *the life (the animal soul) is in the blood*, and I have given it for you upon the altar to make *atonement for your souls*; for it is the blood that makes atonement, by reason of the life (which represents).'(Lev 17:11AMP) [14]"for *it (blood) is the life of all flesh. Its blood sustains its life*. Therefore I said to the children of Israel, 'You shall not eat the blood of any flesh, for *the life of all flesh is its blood*. Whoever eats it shall be cut off.'(Lev 17:14) [23]"Only be sure that you do not eat the blood, *for the blood is the life; you may not eat the life with the meat*.(Deut 12:23)

Saving of the Soul the Seat of Our Person

We May Not Know the Things of God If We Discern Solely by Our Flesh and Blood (Body and Soul): ¹⁴I will praise You, for I am fearfully and wonderfully made; marvelous are Your works, and *that my soul knows very well.*(Ps 139:14) ³"Every moving thing that lives shall be food for you. I have given you all things, even as the green herbs. ⁴"But you shall not eat *flesh with its life, that is, its blood.*(Gen 9:3-4) ¹⁷Jesus answered and said to him, "Blessed are you, Simon Bar-Jonah, for *flesh and blood has not revealed this to you*, but My Father who is in heaven.(Matt 16:17) ⁵⁰Now this I say, brethren, that *flesh and blood cannot inherit the kingdom of God*; nor does corruption inherit incorruption.(1 Cor 15:50) ¹²For we do not wrestle against *flesh and blood*, but against principalities, against powers, against the rulers of the darkness of this age, against spiritual hosts of wickedness in the heavenly places.(Eph 6:12)

Reactive Response of Our Soul for Issues of Life

The Life (Soul) for Discernment for the Scorn and Contempt of Others: ⁶My soul has dwelt too long with one who hates peace.(Ps 120:6) ⁴*Our soul is exceedingly filled with the scorn of those who are at ease, with the contempt of the proud.*(Ps 123:4) ⁵Then *the swollen waters would have gone over our soul."*(Ps 124:5) ¹²They reward me evil for good, *to the sorrow of my soul.*(Ps 35:12) ⁴Look on my right hand and see, for there is no one who acknowledges me; refuge has failed me; *no one cares for my soul.*(Ps 142:4) ⁴Then the waters would have overwhelmed us, *the stream would have gone over our soul*;(Ps 124:4) ²How long shall I *take counsel in my soul*, having sorrow in my heart daily? How long will my enemy be exalted over me?(Ps 13:2) ⁷*Return to your rest, O my soul*, for the LORD has dealt bountifully with you.(Ps 116:7) ¹⁷Unless the LORD had been my help, *my soul would soon have settled in silence.*(Ps 94:17) ¹In the LORD I put my trust; *how can you say to my soul*, "Flee as a bird to your mountain"?(Ps 11:1) ⁷*Our soul has escaped* as a bird from the snare of the fowlers; the snare is broken, and we have escaped.(Ps 124:7)

The Life (Soul) for Discernment for Our Troubles: ²⁶They mount up to the heavens, they go down again to the depths; *their soul melts because of trouble.*(Ps 107:26) ²⁵For *our soul is bowed down to the dust*; our body clings to the ground.(Ps 44:25) ³For *my soul is full of troubles*, and my life draws near to the grave.(Ps 88:3) ²In the day of my trouble I sought the Lord; my hand was stretched out in the night without ceasing; *my soul refused to be comforted.*(Ps 77:2) ³*My soul also is greatly troubled*; but You, O LORD-- how long?(Ps 6:3) ⁵*Why are you cast down, O my soul? And why are you disquieted within me? Hope in God*, for I shall yet praise Him for the help of His countenance.(Ps 42:5) ¹¹*Why are you cast down, O my soul? And why are you disquieted within me? Hope in God*; for I shall yet praise Him, the help of my countenance and my God.(Ps 42:11) ²*Surely I have calmed and quieted my soul*, like a weaned child with his mother; like a weaned child is my soul within me.(Ps 131:2)

The Life (Soul) for Discernment for Our Hunger and Thirst and Our Satisfaction When We Are Fed and Quenched: ¹⁵Notwithstanding thou mayest kill and eat flesh in all thy gates, *whatsoever thy soul lusteth after*, according to the blessing of the LORD thy God which he hath given thee: the unclean and the clean *may eat thereof*, as of the roebuck, and as of the hart.¹⁶Only ye shall not eat the blood; ye shall pour it upon the earth as water.(Deut 12:15-16KJV) ⁷All the labor of man is for his mouth, and *yet the soul is* *not satisfied.*(Eccl 6:7) ⁵*My soul shall be satisfied as with marrow and fatness*, and my mouth shall praise You with joyful lips.(Ps 63:5) ⁷*A satisfied soul loathes the honeycomb*, but to *a hungry soul every bitter thing is sweet.*(Prov 27:7) ⁵*Hungry and thirsty, their soul fainted in them.*(Ps 107:5) ³⁰Men do not despise a thief, if he steals *to satisfy his soul when he is hungry*;(Prov 6:30KJV) ¹⁸*Their soul abhorred all manner of food*, and they drew near to the gates of death.(Ps 107:18) ²⁰So that his life abhors bread, and *his soul succulent food.*(Job 33:20) ⁷*My soul refuses to touch them*; they are as loathsome food to me.(Job 6:7) ¹⁰When I wept and *chastened my soul with fasting*, that became my reproach.(Ps 69:10) ²⁵"Therefore I say to you, *do not worry about your life*, what you will eat or what you will drink; nor about your body, what you will put on. *Is not life more than food* and the body more than clothing?(Matt 6:25)

The Body Dies When Our Soul Departs and Gets Resurrected When Our Soul Comes Back: ¹⁸And so it was, *as her soul was departing (for she died)*, that she called his name Ben-Oni; but his father called him Benjamin.(Gen 35:18) ¹⁹And he said to her, "Give me your son." So he took him out of her arms and carried him to the upper room where he was staying, and laid him on his own bed. ²⁰Then he cried out to the LORD and said, "O LORD my God, have You also brought tragedy on the widow with whom I lodge, by killing her son?" ²¹And he stretched himself out on the child three times, and cried out to the LORD and said, "O LORD my God, I pray, *let this child's soul come back to him.*" ²²Then the LORD heard the voice of Elijah; and *the soul of the child came back to him*, and he revived. ²³And Elijah took the child and brought him down from the upper room into the house, and gave him to his mother. And Elijah said, "See, your son lives!"(IKing 17:19-23)

Destiny of Human Soul

All of Our Souls Are Lost and Abide in Death in Regard to God: ⁴"Behold, all souls are Mine; the soul of the father as well as the soul of the son is Mine; *the soul who sins shall die.*(Ezek 18:4) ¹²Therefore, just as through one man sin entered the world, and death through sin, and *thus death spread to all men*, because all sinned. (Rom 5:12) ²⁴But He (Jesus) answered and said, "I was not sent except to the lost sheep of the house of Israel."(Matt 15:24)

Jesus Is Our Truth and the Life Through His Flesh and Blood: ⁴But He answered and said, "It is written, 'Man shall not live by bread alone, but by every word that proceeds from the mouth of God.'"(Matt 4:4) ¹⁴And the *Word became flesh* and dwelt among us, and we beheld His glory, the glory as of the only begotten of the Father, full of grace and truth.(John 1:14) ⁶Jesus said to him, "*I am the way, the truth, and the life*"(John 14:6) Indeed ⁵⁴"*Whoever eats My flesh and drinks My blood has eternal life.*(John 6:54) ¹¹For the *life of the flesh is in the blood*, and I have given it to you upon the altar to make atonement for your souls; for *it is the blood that makes <u>atonement for the soul</u>.*'(Lev 17:11)

The Soul Continues to Exist either in Heaven or Hell After It Leaves the Body: ²⁷For *You will not leave my soul in Hades*, nor will You allow Your Holy One to see corruption.(Acts 2:27) ⁹When He opened the fifth seal, *I saw under the altar the souls* of those who had been slain for the word of God and for the testimony which they held.(Rev

$_{6:9)}$ ^{20}"But God said to him, 'Fool! *This night your soul will be required of you*; then whose will those things be which you have provided?'$_{(Luke\ 12:20)}$ ^{28}"And do not fear those who kill the body but *cannot kill the soul*. But rather fear Him who is *able to destroy both soul and body in hell*.$_{(Matt\ 10:28)}$ ^{50}He made a path for His anger; *he did not spare their soul from death*, but gave their life over to the plague.$_{(Ps\ 78:50)}$

Jesus Saves Our Souls

We Can Enter Through Jesus and Be Saved: Jesus said ^{9}"*I am the door. If anyone enters by Me, he will be saved*, and will go in and out and find pasture.$_{(John\ 10:9)}$ ^{36}"Therefore *if the Son makes you free, you shall be free indeed*.$_{(John\ 8:36)}$ ^{31}Then Jesus said to those Jews who believed Him, "If you abide in My word, you are My disciples indeed. ^{32}"And *you shall know the truth, and the truth shall make you free*." $_{(John\ 8:31-32)}$ Therefore ^{28}"Come to Me, all you who labor and are heavy laden, and I will give you rest. ^{29}"Take My yoke upon you and learn from Me, for I am gentle and lowly in heart, and *you will find rest for your souls*. ^{30}"For My yoke is easy and My burden is light."$_{(Matt\ 11:28-30)}$ ^{51}"Most assuredly, I say to you, *if anyone keeps My word he shall never see death*."$_{(John\ 8:51)}$

Salvation in Jesus Name Through Love and Faith: ^{12}"Nor is there salvation in any other, for there is *no other name under heaven given among men by which we must be saved*."$_{(Acts\ 4:12)}$ ^{23}And this is His commandment: that *we should believe on the name of His Son Jesus Christ and love one another*, as He gave us commandment. ^{24}Now he who keeps His commandments abides in Him, and He in him. And by this we know that He abides in us, by the Spirit whom He has given us.$_{(I\ Jn\ 3:23-24)}$ For ^{36}"He *who believes in the Son has everlasting life*; and he who does not believe the Son shall not see life, but the wrath of God abides on him."$_{(John\ 3:36)}$ ^{31}but these are written that you may believe that Jesus is the Christ, the Son of God, and that *believing you may have life in His name*.$_{(John\ 20:31)}$ ^{11}And this is the testimony: that God has given us eternal life, and this life is in His Son. ^{12}He who has the Son has life; he who does not have the Son of God does not have life. ^{13}These things I have written to you who believe in the name of the Son of God, that you may know that you have eternal life, and that *you may continue to believe in the name of the Son of God*.$_{(I\ Jn\ 5:11-13)}$

Salvation of Our Soul by the Word and the Spirit

Salvation of Our Soul in Jesus by the Implanted Word of God: ^{24}"to testify to *the gospel of the grace of God*.$_{(Acts\ 20:24)}$ ^{5}you heard before in the word of the truth of the gospel, ^{6}which has come to you, as it has also in all the world, and is bringing forth fruit, as it is also among you since the day you heard and knew the grace of God in truth;$_{(Col\ 1:5-6)}$ Then ^{21}receive with meekness *the implanted word, which is able to save your souls*.$_{(James\ 1:21)}$ ^{17}So then faith comes by hearing, and hearing by the word of God.$_{(Rom\ 10:17)}$ and by ^{9}receiving *the end of your faith-- the salvation of your souls*. ^{10}Of this salvation the prophets have inquired and searched carefully, who prophesied of the grace that would come to you.$_{(1\ Pet\ 1:9-10)}$ For ^{11}"we believe that *through the grace of the Lord Jesus Christ we shall be saved*."$_{(Acts\ 15:11)}$ ^{8}*For by grace you have been saved through faith*, and that not of ourselves; it is the gift of God.$_{(Eph\ 2:8)}$ ^{31}Then Jesus said to those Jews who believed Him, "If you abide in My word, you are My disciples indeed. ³²"And ***you shall know the truth, and the truth shall make you free.***"(John 8:31-32) ²⁴"Most assuredly, I say to you, ***he who hears My word and believes in Him who sent Me has everlasting life***, and shall not come into judgment, but has passed from death into life.(John 5:24)

We Cannot Confess Jesus Is Lord and Be Saved Without the Help of the Holy Spirit: ¹³God from the beginning chose you for ***salvation through sanctification by the Spirit and belief in the truth***, ¹⁴to which He called you by our gospel.(II Th 2:13-14) ⁵For our gospel did not come to you in word only, but also in power, and in the Holy Spirit and in much assurance.(1Thes 1:5) ¹²through those ***who have preached the gospel to you by the Holy Spirit*** sent from heaven.(1 Pet 1:12) ³Therefore I make known to you that no one speaking by the Spirit of God calls Jesus accursed, and ***no one can say that Jesus is Lord except by the Holy Spirit***.(1 Cor 12:3) ¹³And since we have the same ***spirit of faith***, according to what is written, "I believed and therefore I spoke," we also believe and therefore speak.(2 Cor 4:13) ¹⁷where the Spirit of the Lord is, there is liberty.(2 Cor 3:17) Jesus said ¹³"However, when He, the Spirit of truth, has come, He will guide you into all truth. (John 16:13) ¹⁷"He who has an ear, let him hear what the Spirit says to the churches. To him who overcomes I will give some of the hidden manna to eat.(Rev 2:17) ¹¹"He who overcomes shall not be hurt by the second death."(Rev 2:11) ²²Since you have ***purified your souls in obeying the truth through the Spirit*** in sincere love of the brethren.(1 Pet 1:22)

When We Call Upon the Name of the Lord and Confess Jesus with Our Mouth We Will Be Saved: ¹⁷So then faith comes by hearing, and hearing by the word of God.(Rom 10:17) ⁸But what does it say? "The word is near you, in your mouth and in your heart" (that is, the word of faith which we preach): ⁹that ***if you confess with your mouth the Lord Jesus and believe in your heart that God has raised Him from the dead, you will be saved***. ¹⁰For with the heart one believes unto righteousness, and with the mouth confession is made unto salvation. ¹¹For the Scripture says, "Whoever believes on Him will not be put to shame." ¹²For there is no distinction between Jew and Greek, for the same Lord over all is rich to all who call upon Him. ¹³For "whoever calls on the name of the Lord shall be saved."(Rom 10:8-13) For ²¹Death and life are in the power of the tongue, and those who love it will eat its fruit.(Prov 18:21)

Forfeiting the Salvation Through Unbelief

We May Not Profit From the Gospel If We Do Not Mix Faith with It: ²For indeed the gospel was preached to us as well as to them; but ***the word which they heard did not profit them, not being mixed with faith in those who heard it***. ³For we who have believed do enter that rest, as He has said: "So I swore in My wrath, they shall not enter My rest," although the works were finished from the foundation of the world.(Heb 4:2-3) ¹⁸And to whom did He swear that they would not enter His rest, but to those who did not obey? ¹⁹So we see that ***they could not enter in because of unbelief***.(Heb 3:18-19) ¹²Beware, brethren, lest there be in any of you an ***evil heart of unbelief*** in departing from the living God; ¹³but exhort one another daily, while it is called "Today," lest any of you ***be hardened through the deceitfulness of sin***.(Heb 3:12-13)

The Heart Our Inner Processing Center

The heart is the central part of a human being. It reveals the real person as a mirror reflects our face. What we treasure in our heart shows our true character. The human heart is deep and out of it springs the issues of life. Counsel in our heart is like deep water and the people of understanding will draw it out. We comprehend the spiritual as well as the natural discernment for issues of life by our heart. We therefore coordinate, integrate and regulate the activities of the spirit and body in our heart. We know in our heart the willingness or resistance, emotions, passions and appetites of our soul. They include love or hate; joy or sorrow; peace or anger/bitterness; courage or fear and more.

The heart of a human may be thought of as a CPU (central processing unit) in any equipment, which employs computers. The equipment usually consists of speakers, displays, warning signals, sensors and moving parts. The sensors may include cameras for the sight, microphones for the sound, thermometers for the temperature, compass for direction, pieces that measure wind speed, altitude etc. The CPU coordinates the commands input by the operator, incorporates the data acquired by the sensors and executes the programs stored in the memory units. The CPU also regulates the moving parts to get the work done according to the will of the operator. The freewill choices stem from our proactive response ability of our soul could be compared with the commands of the operator. The sensors are like our senses. The emotions result from our reactive response ability of our soul are like unto the reactions of the operator to the CPU findings. The software programs in the memory usually work according to the laws pertaining to the issue at hand. This could be compared with the laws written in our heart that we employ to reason the ongoing issue.

If we like to understand an issue, first we gather the knowledge about that topic and meditate in our heart what we know. Gathering knowledge is analogous to feeding all the data acquired by sensors of equipment to the CPU. The activities such as communing with our hearts, saying in our hearts, reasoning in our hearts, all contribute to our mediation. In other words, when we apply our heart to instruction and knowledge regard to that issue, we gain understanding. These are similar to entering commands and running relevant software programs that execute all logical sequence of the required laws or principles on the data. The result output by CPU may enable us to gain understanding. It also

Gaining Your Ability to Interact with God

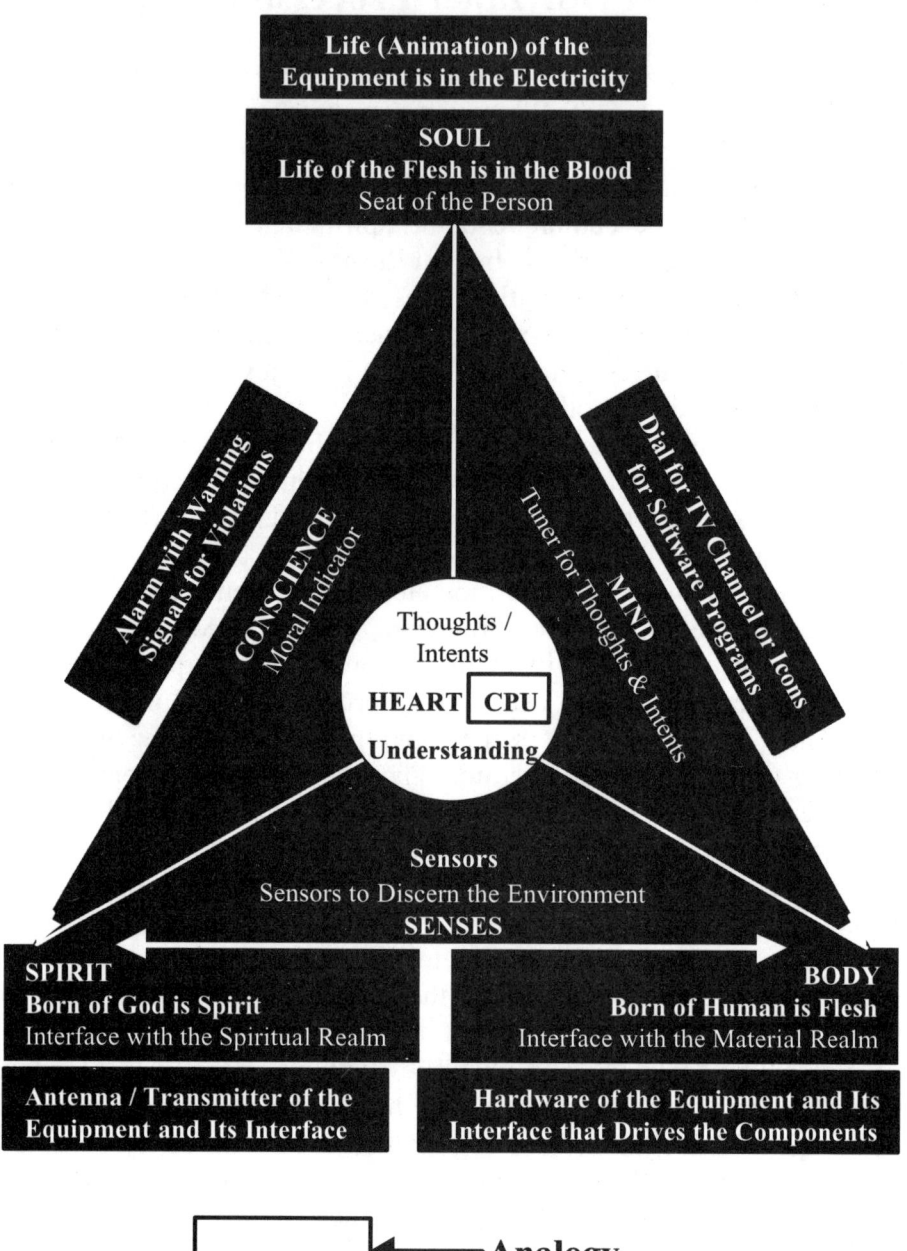

Analogy for the Heart of Humankind

helps us to make wise conclusions and recommendations. For example, applying the knowledge of the word of God to the heart helps us to understand the issues of life. We may readily discern good and evil by knowing the intent behind our daily encounters. The inward knowing usually stirs up either uplifting or wounding emotions in our heart for various issues of life. If we are of wise heart we may be called prudent. For we receive God's commands and let our heart teach our mouth what to say. Wisdom will be found in our lips if we speak from an understanding heart. As a result, we may be able to hold our peace and go in the way of understanding. This to us is a well spring of life that leads to the destiny God has for us.

The visual summary for the make-up of human being together with the analogy is reproduced on the page to the left. The summary for the heart and the corresponding analogy (CPU) are highlighted inside the center circle. As shown within the highlighted area, we **understand** the issues of life by applying the heart to the knowledge and instruction. Also, we set our ***thoughts and intents*** in our heart for the steps of our life.

Now we consider some of the phrases used in the Bible to understand how our heart like a mirror reflects our emotional reactions. The following are some biblical phrases for uplifting emotions. My heart will rejoice for I refresh my heart in the LORD. God fills our heart with food and gladness. A merry heart does good like medicine. Therefore, my heart rejoices in the LORD. The following are some biblical phrases for hurting emotions. The heart knows its own bitterness. My heart is wounded within me. My heart is severely pained within me. My heart is like wax, it has melted within me. I groan because of the turmoil of my heart. My heart is stricken and withered like grass. My heart is hot within me. I have great sorrow and continual grief in my heart. In the anguish of my heart I wrote to you. I am fearful hearted. Let not your heart be troubled, believe in God.

The counsel in our heart for our daily decisions is greatly influenced by our beliefs and values. The laws written in our heart essentially reflect the principles we live by. We, in our heart, set the thoughts and intentions for the steps of our life. If we set our motives to love God and others with our heart, faith, purity, sincerity; and maturity -- all these would be the condition of our heart. We may spontaneously make all our decisions by faith on God's Word. These choices empower us to prosper through the pursuit of God given vision. The grace of God that abounds towards us

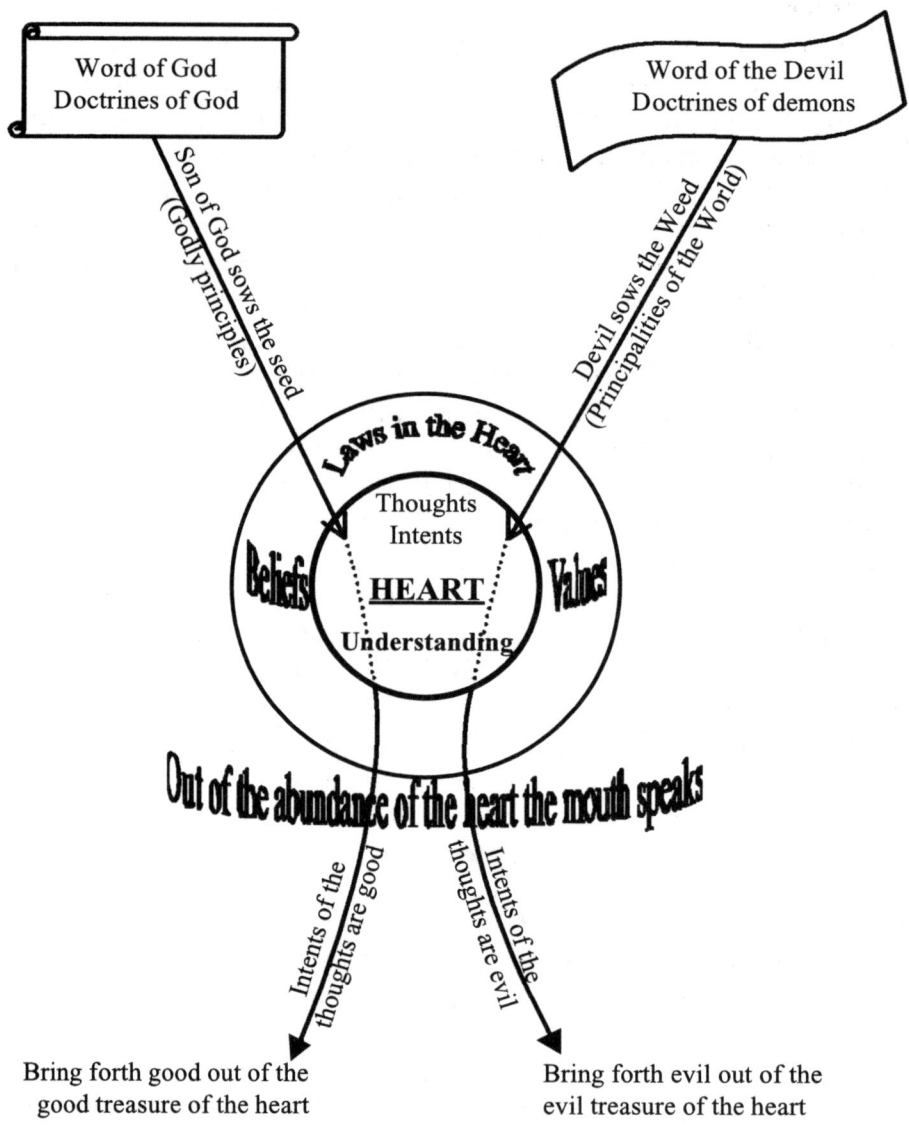

Role of the Human Heart in Character Development

through our right standing with God by faith issues all that are necessary for our life. Provision by God's grace to pursue the vision and reap the fruits brings fulfillment to our inner desire to prosper.

Our heart is like the ground that can either receive the seed or the weed sown into it. It will let them grow and mature in due season. Faith comes by hearing, hearing by the word. Therefore, what we willingly hear and trust becomes our beliefs and values. They are like the laws written in our hearts. The belief system that is built according to the promises and principles becomes the foundation for our life. Whereas, what we treasure in our heart shapes our value system. It will be reflected by our priorities. Consequently, out of the abundance (treasures) of our heart our mouth will speak.

Son of God is He who sows the incorruptible seed, the word of God, in our hearts. If we keep our patience while we run the race of faith, we will bear fruits from the seed. For the seed takes root and becomes our beliefs and values rooted in the doctrines of God. As a result, the laws written in our hearts will reflect godly principles. We will start treasuring in our hearts the things of God and His kingdom. Our intents will be centered on loving God that manifest through our service and worship of God. Since, Jesus is the rock of all ages and the very embodiment of the word of God, we will build our life on that rock that cannot be shaken. The thoughts that result from the indwelling word will be good. They will be filled with love, faith, hope and fear of God. We know that out of the abundance of the heart our mouth speaks. We will therefore bring forth good out of the good treasure of our heart for the glory of God.

On the contrary, the devil sows the corruptible weeds in our hearts that are contrary to the word of God. They certainly appeal to our natural senses. We may become devil's children, if we let these doctrines of demons take root and remain in our heart. For they turn into our beliefs and values over a period of time. Consequently, we will start treasuring in our hearts the things of the spirit of this world. What we treasure will be evident by our intents that are usually centered on the service and worship of idols. As a result, our thoughts will be evil and be filled with pride, lust, idols and fear of death. Out of the abundance of the heart our mouth speaks. We will therefore, for our disgrace, bring forth evil out of the evil treasure of our heart.

The visual summary on the page to the left shows the two scenarios described above. The left half summarizes our condition when we let the seed, the doctrines of God take root. The seed in this case is the word of

God. The right half shows what happens to us when we let the weed, doctrines of demons, grow in our hearts. As shown along the two arrows approaching the center circles from the top on page 88, the Son of God sows the seed and the devil sows the weed in our hearts. The laws in the heart, shown inside the circular annulus on page 88, regulate our logical reasoning. The beliefs and values, shown inside the same circular annulus, reflect what we treasure in our heart. As shown immediately below the outer circle on page 88, out of the abundance (treasures) of our heart the mouth speaks. Our intents of the thoughts are going to be either good or evil, as shown along the two arrows below the center circles, depending on whether we are God's or devil's children. The type of fruits we bring forth in life are going to be determined by the kind of treasure in our heart, as stated at the tail end of the arrows at the bottom of the diagram on page 88.

In a TV telecast, three kinds of information are used to communicate the plan and purposes of the producer (author) of the programs. These are light of the knowledge of the glory of the images, words and sounds (noise/music). They show forth the will and emotions in regard to the plan and purposes of the originator of the programs. Similarly, thoughts of our hearts also carry three kinds of information. These are light of the knowledge of the glory of God, people and things (images), words (principles) and emotions (noises/music).

We have three options to base our walk in life. They are either life according to Spirit or flesh or world. Life according to the flesh and the world are contrary to the life according to the spirit. We may choose to walk according to the flesh or world by not yielding to the Spirit of God.

Now, we consider the life according to the flesh. We will be cursed, if we trust in people and make the flesh our strength. In this scenario, we may have an uncircumcised heart. Our heart in this condition is deceitful above all things, and desperately wicked, who can know it. For the intents will be centered on serving and worshipping us as our own Lord. The intent of the thoughts of our heart will therefore be only evil and be rooted in pride, lust, idols and fear of people.

On the other hand, we may choose to walk according to the course of this world, according to the prince of the power of the air. This spirit works now in the sons of disobedience. In this scenario, we may have the spirit of the world in our heart. This condition helps Satan to easily snatch away the word of the kingdom of God, as soon as it is sown in our heart. If we let Satan fill our heart, we may lie to the Holy Spirit, for he blinds our heart to the understanding of the truth. We may exhibit a nature that belongs to children of wrath. As a result, intents and thoughts of our hearts may be rooted in pride, lust, idols and fear of death, according to this world.

God through prophet Ezekial promised us a new heart and a new spirit and also His Spirit within us. Jesus said that we couldn't enter and see the kingdom of God without receiving this promise. If we indeed get a new heart and a new spirit by faith in Jesus, we may receive the gift of the Spirit of God in our heart. We who search our hearts know what the mind of the Spirit is. For He makes intercession for us according to the will, plans and purposes of God. Consequently, we may be able to know the things that have been freely given to us by God. Also, the circumcision that is of the heart in the spirit helps us to love God with our heart and soul. For the Holy Spirit has poured out the love of God in our hearts. As a result, intents and thoughts of our hearts may be rooted in love, faith, hope and fear of God. We may therefore keep God's judgments and do them.

God is light and was Word. The entrance of the Word brings light. The light that brings understanding to the heart enables God's people to effectively interact with a good God, an evil Satan and other objects of God's creation. God is love. God pours out His love in the heart of His people by His Spirit. People who walk with God may therefore be able to yield to His love. They have capacity to make decisions by faith to love God, people and other God's creatures. Though the preparation of the heart belongs to us the answer of the tongue is from the LORD. We may make many plans in our heart to fulfill the purpose, however, only the LORD'S counsel that will stand. In other words, the LORD directs our steps though our heart plans the way. Therefore, we have to trust in the Lord and not lean on our own understanding.

A visual summary for the primary attributes of our heart is presented on next page. As shown within the center circle of the diagram, thoughts with certain intents are invariably inspired in our hearts. They help us to understand the issues of life. These thoughts and intents, as shown within the inner circular annulus on next page, originate from three distinctive sources known as Spirit, flesh and world. Also, these thoughts of our hearts carry three kinds of information, as described within the outer circular annulus on next page. These are images (light of the knowledge of the glory of God, people and things), words (principles) and emotions (noises/music). We in our heart may either be uncircumcised or have the

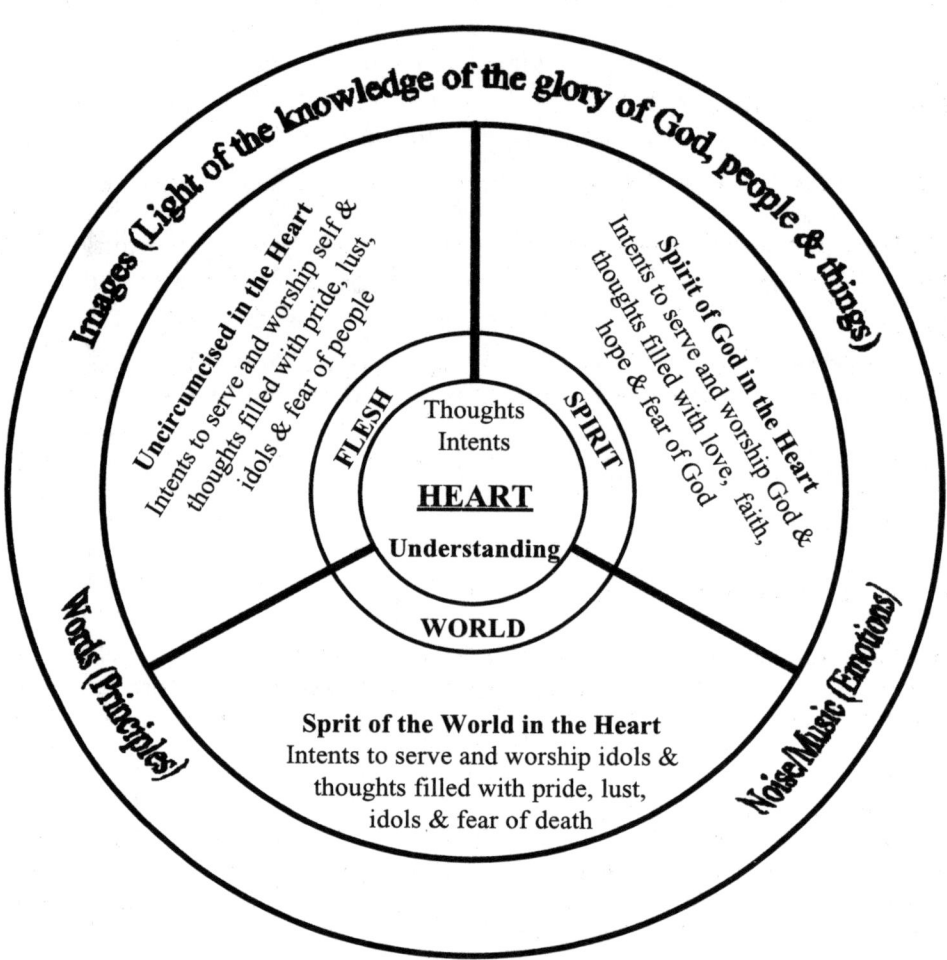

Primary Attributes of the Human Heart

spirit of the world or the Spirit of God. The status of our heart results from each condition is summarized separately inside the three sectors located between inner and outer circular annulus of the diagram on the page to the left.

Bible References

Heart Is the Central Part of Human

The Issues of Our Life Proceed Out of Our Heart: ^{19}As in water face reflects face, so a man's heart reveals the man.(Prov 27:19) ^{7}For as he thinks in his heart, so is he. "Eat and drink!" he says to you, but his heart is not with you. (Prov 23:7) ^{23}Keep your heart with all diligence, for out of it spring the issues of life.(Prov 4:23) ^{6}Both the inward thought and the heart of man are deep.(Ps 64:6) ^{5}Counsel in the heart of man is like deep water, but a man of understanding will draw it out.(Prov 20:5) ^{45}"A good man out of the good treasure of his heart brings forth good; and an evil man out of the evil treasure of his heart brings forth evil. For out of the abundance of the heart his mouth speaks.(Luke 6:45). ^{19}"For out of the heart proceed evil thoughts, murders, adulteries, fornications, thefts, false witness, blasphemies.(Matt 15:19)

Intents and Thoughts of the Human Heart

We Plan and Purpose in Our Hearts According to the Intents and Thoughts of Our Hearts: ^{5}Then the LORD saw that the wickedness of man was great in the earth, and that *every intent of the thoughts of his heart was only evil continually*.(Gen 6:5) ^{12}For the *word of God* is living and powerful, and sharper than any two-edged sword, piercing even to the division of soul and spirit, and of joints and marrow, and *is a discerner of the thoughts and intents of the heart*.(Heb 4:12) ^{9}*A man's heart plans his way*, but the LORD directs his steps.(Prov 16:9) ^{4}Now it happened after this that Joash *set his heart on repairing the house of the LORD*.(2 Chr 24:4) ^{1}*The preparations of the heart belong to man*, but the answer of the tongue is from the LORD.(Prov 16:1) ^{21}*There are many plans in a man's heart*, nevertheless the LORD'S counsel-- that will stand.(Prov 19:21) ^{23}When he came and had seen the grace of God, he was glad, and encouraged them all that *with purpose of heart they should continue with the Lord*.(Acts 11:23) ^{7}So *let each one give as he purposes in his heart*, not grudgingly or of necessity; for God loves a cheerful giver. (2 Cor 9:7) ^{12}I am sending him back. You therefore receive him, *that is, my own heart*.(Phile 1:12)

We Can Reason and Understand Using Our Inner Thoughts: ^{6}And some of the scribes were sitting there and *reasoning in their hearts*.(Mark 2:6) ^{31}"So they come to you as people do, they sit before you as My people, and they hear your words, but they do not do them; *for with their mouth they show much love, but their hearts pursue their own gain*.(Ezek 33:31) ^{19}O my soul, my soul! *I am pained in my very heart! My heart makes a noise in me*; I cannot hold my peace, because you have heard, O my soul, the sound of the trumpet, the alarm of war.(Jer 4:19) ^{17}Then Abraham fell on his face and laughed, and *said in his heart*, "Shall a child be born to a man who is one hundred years old? And shall Sarah, who is ninety years old, bear a child?"(Gen 17:17) ¹⁶*I communed with my heart*, saying, "Look, I have attained greatness, and have gained more wisdom than all who were before me in Jerusalem. *My heart has understood great wisdom and knowledge.*" ¹⁷And *I set my heart to know wisdom and to know madness and folly. I perceived* that this also is grasping for the wind.(Eccl 1:16-17)

Understanding by the Human Heart

We Understand by Applying Our Heart to the Knowledge: ³My mouth shall speak wisdom, and *the meditation of my heart shall give understanding*.(Ps 49:3) ¹*My heart is overflowing with a good theme*; I recite my composition concerning the King; my tongue is the pen of a ready writer.(Ps 45:1) ⁵O you simple ones, understand prudence, and you fools, *be of an understanding heart*.(Prov 8:5) ²⁶*My son, give me your heart*, and let your eyes observe my ways.(Prov 23:26) ¹²*Apply your heart to instruction*, and your ears to words of knowledge.(Prov 23:12) ¹⁷Incline your ear and hear the words of the wise, and *apply your heart to my knowledge*;(Prov 22:17) ¹My son, if you receive my words, and treasure my commands within you, ²So that you incline your ear to wisdom, and *apply your heart to understanding*; (Prov 2:1-2) ³³*Wisdom rests in the heart of him who has understanding*, but what is in the heart of fools is made known.(Prov 14:33) ²¹*The wise in heart will be called prudent*, and sweetness of the lips increases learning. ²²*Understanding is a wellspring of life to him who has it*. But the correction of fools is folly. ²³*The heart of the wise teaches his mouth*, and adds learning to his lips.(Prov 16:21-23)

Wisdom in Living in the Way of Understanding: ¹⁹Hear, my son, and *be wise; and guide your heart in the way*.(Prov 23:19) ¹²He who is devoid of wisdom despises his neighbor, but *a man of understanding holds his peace*.(Prov 11:12) ⁶Forsake foolishness and live, and *go in the way of understanding*.(Prov 9:6) ¹¹Discretion will preserve you; *understanding will keep you*.(Prov 2:11)

We Can Understand the Uplifting Emotions by Our Heart: ⁹Therefore *my heart is glad*, and my glory rejoices; my flesh also will rest in hope.(Ps 16:9) ²²*A merry heart does good*, like medicine, but a broken spirit dries the bones.(Prov 17:22) ¹⁵My son, *if your heart is wise, my heart will rejoice*-- indeed, I myself;(Prov 23:15) ²⁰Yes, brother, let me have joy from you in the Lord; *refresh my heart* in the Lord.(Phile 1:20) ¹⁷"Nevertheless He did not leave Himself without witness, in that He did good, gave us rain from heaven and fruitful seasons, *filling our hearts with food and gladness*."(Acts 14:17) ¹And Hannah prayed and said: "*My heart rejoices in the LORD*; my horn is exalted in the LORD. I smile at my enemies, because I rejoice in Your salvation.(1 Sam 2:1)

We Can Understand the Wounding Emotions by Our Heart: ¹⁰*The heart knows its own bitterness*, and a stranger does not share its joy.(Prov 14:10) ²²For I am poor and needy, and *my heart is wounded within me*.(Ps 109:22) ⁴*My heart is severely pained within me*, and the terrors of death have fallen upon me.(Ps 55:4) ¹⁴I am poured out like water, and all My bones are out of joint; *my heart is like wax; it has melted within Me*.(Ps 22:14) ⁸I am feeble and severely broken; I groan because of *the turmoil of my heart*.(Ps 38:8) ⁴*My heart* *is stricken and withered like grass*, so that I forget to eat my bread.(Ps 102:4) ²I was mute with silence, I held my peace even from good; and my sorrow was stirred up. ³*My heart was hot within me*; while I was musing, the fire burned. Then I spoke with my tongue:(Ps 39:2-3) ²that *I have great sorrow and continual grief in my heart*.(Rom 9:2) ⁴For out of much affliction and *anguish of heart* I wrote to you, with many tears, not that you should be grieved, but that you might know the love which I have so abundantly for you.(2 Cor 2:4) ⁴Say to those who are *fearful-hearted*, "Be strong, do not fear! Behold, your God will come with vengeance, with the recompense of God; he will come and save you."(Isa 35:4) ¹"*Let not your heart be troubled*; you believe in God, believe also in Me.(John 14:1) ²²"Therefore you now have sorrow; but I will see you again and *your heart will rejoice*, and your joy no one will take from you.(John 16:22)

Knowing People by the Fruit from the Word in Their Heart

Word of the Kingdom Is Sown in Our Hearts to Bear Fruit for God: ¹⁸"Therefore hear the parable of the sower: ¹⁹"When anyone hears *the word of the kingdom*, and does not understand it, then the wicked one comes and snatches away *what was sown in his heart*. This is he who *received seed* by the wayside. ²⁰"But he who received the seed on stony places, this is he who hears the word and immediately receives it with joy; ²¹"yet he has no root in himself, but endures only for a while. For when tribulation or persecution arises because of the word, immediately he stumbles. ²²"Now he who received seed among the thorns is he who hears the word, and the cares of this world and the deceitfulness of riches choke the word, and he becomes unfruitful. ²³"But he who received seed on the good ground is he who hears the word and understands it, who indeed bears fruit and produces: some a hundredfold, some sixty, some thirty."(Matt 13:18-23)

Jesus and the Devil Sowing the Seed and the Tares (Weed), Respectively: ³⁶Then Jesus sent the multitude away and went into the house. And His disciples came to Him, saying, "Explain to us the parable of the tares of the field." ³⁷He answered and said to them: "*He who sows the good seed is the Son of Man*. ³⁸"*The field is the world, the good seeds are the sons of the kingdom, but the tares are the sons of the wicked one*. ³⁹"*The enemy who sowed them is the devil*, the harvest is the end of the age, and the reapers are the angels. ⁴⁰"Therefore as the tares are gathered and burned in the fire, so it will be at the end of this age. ⁴¹"The Son of Man will send out His angels, and they will gather out of His kingdom all things that offend, and those who practice lawlessness, ⁴²"and will cast them into the furnace of fire. There will be wailing and gnashing of teeth. ⁴³"Then the righteous will shine forth as the sun in the kingdom of their Father. He who has ears to hear, let him hear!(Matt 13:36-43)

Condition of the Uncircumcised Heart

Prideful and Lustful and Idolatrous Intents of the Heart of a Natural Man: ¹⁶I say then: Walk in the Spirit, and you shall not fulfill the lust of the flesh.(Gal 5:16) ¹⁴But *the natural man does not receive the things of the Spirit of God*, for they are foolishness to him; nor can he know them, *because they are spiritually discerned*.(1 Cor 2:14) For ¹⁵"You judge according to the flesh.(John 8:15) and therefore ¹⁴*have a heart trained in covetous*

practices.(2 Pet 2:14) [4]God is wise in heart and mighty in strength. Who has hardened himself against Him and prospered?(Job 9:4) [20]"But when ***his heart was lifted up***, and his spirit was hardened in pride, he was deposed from his kingly throne, and they took his glory from him.(Dan 5:20) [5]But in accordance with your ***hardness and your impenitent heart*** you are treasuring up for yourself wrath in the day of wrath and revelation of the righteous judgment of God.(Rom 2:5) [12]"Yes, ***they made their hearts like flint, refusing to hear the law and the words which the LORD of hosts had sent by His Spirit through the former prophets***. Thus great wrath came from the LORD of hosts.[13]"Therefore it happened, that just as He proclaimed and they would not hear, so they called out and I would not listen,"says the LORD of hosts.(Zech 7:12-13) [21]Although they knew God, they did not glorify Him as God, nor were thankful, but became futile in their thoughts, and ***their foolish hearts were darkened***. [22]Professing to be wise, they became fools, [23]and changed the glory of the incorruptible God into an image made like corruptible man-- and birds and four-footed animals and creeping things. [24]Therefore ***God also gave them up to uncleanness, in the lusts of their hearts***, to dishonor their bodies among themselves, [25]who exchanged the truth of God for the lie, and ***worshipped and served the creature rather than the Creator***, who is blessed forever. Amen. (Rom 1:21-25)

We Can Be Dead in Uncircumcision of Our Heart and Flesh: [9]"Thus says the Lord GOD: "No foreigner, ***uncircumcised in heart*** or uncircumcised in flesh, shall enter My sanctuary.(Ezek 44:9) [13]And you, ***being dead in your trespasses and the uncircumcision of your flesh***, He has made alive together with Him, having forgiven you all trespasses.(Col 2:13) [5]Trust in the LORD with all your heart, and ***lean not on your own understanding***; (Prov 3:5) [5]"***God resists the proud, but gives grace to the humble.***(1 Pet 5:5) [4]Circumcise yourselves to the LORD, and ***take away the foreskins of your hearts***, you men of Judah and inhabitants of Jerusalem, lest My fury come forth like fire, and burn so that no one can quench it, because of the evil of your doings."(Jer 4:4) Jesus said [42]"But I know you, that you do not have the love of God in you.(John 5:42)

We Cannot Love God and Live Without Letting God Circumcise Our Hearts: [11]In Him you were also circumcised with the circumcision made without hands, by putting off the body of the sins of the flesh, by the circumcision of Christ.(Col 2:11) [29]but he is a Jew who is one inwardly; and ***circumcision is that of the heart***, in the Spirit, not in the letter; whose praise is not from men but from God.(Rom 2:29) [3]For we are the circumcision, who worship God in the Spirit, rejoice in Christ Jesus, and have no confidence in the flesh.(Phil 3:3) [16]"Therefore ***circumcise the foreskin of your heart***, and be stiff-necked no longer.(Deut 10:16) [6]"And the ***LORD your God will circumcise your heart and the heart of your descendants***, to love the LORD your God with all your heart and with all your soul, ***that you may live.***(Deut 30:6) [5]because the love of God has been poured out in our hearts by the Holy Spirit who was given to us.(Rom 5:5)

Spirit of the World in the Heart

We May Speak Things Inspired by Satan: [21]From that time Jesus began to show to His disciples that He must go to Jerusalem, and suffer many things from the elders and chief priests and scribes, and be killed, and be raised the third day. [22]Then Peter took Him aside and began to rebuke Him, saying, "Far be it from You, Lord; this shall not

The Heart Our Inner Processing Center

happen to You!" ²³But He turned and said to Peter, "***Get behind Me, Satan! You are an offense to Me***, for you are not mindful of the things of God, but the things of men."(Matt 16:21-23)

Judas Betrayed Jesus Being Filled with Satan: ³*Then Satan entered Judas*, surnamed Iscariot, who was numbered among the twelve. ⁴So he went his way and conferred with the chief priests and captains, how he might betray Him to them. ⁵And they were glad, and agreed to give him money.(Luke 22:3-5) ²¹When Jesus had said these things, He was troubled in spirit, and testified and said, "Most assuredly, I say to you, one of you will betray Me." ²²Then the disciples looked at one another, perplexed about whom He spoke. ²³Now there was leaning on Jesus' bosom one of His disciples, whom Jesus loved. ²⁴Simon Peter therefore motioned to him to ask who it was of whom He spoke. ²⁵Then, leaning back on Jesus' breast, he said to Him, "Lord, who is it?" ²⁶Jesus answered, "It is he to whom I shall give a piece of bread when I have dipped it." And having dipped the bread, He gave it to Judas Iscariot, the son of Simon. ²⁷Now *after the piece of bread, Satan entered him*. Then Jesus said to him, "What you do, do quickly." ²⁸But no one at the table knew for what reason He said this to him.(John 13:21-28)

People May Lie to the Holy Spirit by Letting Satan Fill Their Hearts: ³But Peter said, "***Ananias, why has Satan filled your heart to lie to the Holy Spirit*** and keep back part of the price of the land for yourself? ⁴"While it remained, was it not your own? And after it was sold, was it not in your own control? Why have you conceived this thing in your heart? You have not lied to men but to God."(Acts 5:3-4)

Holy Spirit in and Through Our Heart

We Receive From the LORD a New Heart of Flesh in Place of Heart of Stone and His Spirit Within Us: ²⁵"Then I will sprinkle clean water on you, and you shall be clean; I will cleanse you from all your filthiness and from all your idols. ²⁶"*I will give you a new heart and put a new spirit within you; I will take the heart of stone out of your flesh and give you a heart of flesh*. ²⁷"*I will put My Spirit within you* and cause you to walk in My statutes, and you will keep My judgments and do them. ²⁸"Then you shall dwell in the land that I gave to your fathers; you shall be My people, and I will be your God. ²⁹"I will deliver you from all your uncleannesses.(Ezek 36:25-29)

Holy Spirit in and Through Our Hearts to Those Who Believe in Jesus: Jesus said ³⁸"He who believes in Me, as the Scripture has said, *out of his heart will flow rivers of living water*." ³⁹*But this He spoke concerning the Spirit*, whom those believing in Him would receive.(John 7:38-39) ¹³Christ has redeemed us from the curse of the law, having become a curse for us (for it is written, "Cursed is everyone who hangs on a tree"), ¹⁴that the blessing of Abraham might come upon the Gentiles in Christ Jesus, that *we might receive the promise of the Spirit through faith*.(Gal 3:13-14) ²This only I want to learn from you: Did you receive the Spirit by the works of the law, or by the hearing of faith?(Gal 3:2)

Dominion Over Sin by God's Spirit and Grace: ¹⁴For *sin shall not have dominion over you, for you are not under law but under grace*. ¹⁷But God be thanked that *though you were slaves of sin, yet you obeyed from the heart that form of doctrine to which*

Gaining Your Ability to Interact with God

you were delivered. [18]And having been set free from sin, you became slaves of righteousness.(Rom 6:14,17,18) Therefore [15]until *the Spirit is poured upon us from on high*, and the wilderness becomes a fruitful field, and the fruitful field is counted as a forest. [16]Then justice will dwell in the wilderness, and *righteousness remain in the fruitful field*. [17]The work of righteousness will be peace, and the effect of righteousness, quietness and assurance forever.(Isa 32:15-17) [9](for the fruit of the Spirit is in all goodness, righteousness, and truth).(Eph 5:9) For [17]The kingdom of God is not eating and drinking, but *righteousness and peace and joy in the Holy Spirit*.(Rom 14:17)

The Spirit of God Helps Us to Walk in God's Statutes: [21]There are many plans in a man's heart, nevertheless the LORD'S counsel-- that will stand.(Prov 19:21) [9]A man's heart plans his way, but the LORD directs his steps.(Prov 16:9) [13]"When He, the Spirit of truth, has come, He will guide you into all truth.(John 16:13) [23]And this is God's commandment: that we should believe on the name of His Son Jesus Christ and love one another, as He gave us commandment. [24]Now he who keeps His commandments abides in Him, and He in him. And by this *we know that He abides in us, by the Spirit whom He has given us*.(I Jn 3:23-24)) [5]Now hope does not disappoint, because *the love of God has been poured out in our hearts by the Holy Spirit* who was given to us.(Rom 5:5) For [22]the fruit of the Spirit is love, joy, peace, longsuffering, kindness, goodness, faithfulness, [23]gentleness, self-control. Against such there is no law. [24]And those who are Christ's have crucified the flesh with its passions and desires. [25]*If we live in the Spirit, let us also walk in the Spirit*.(Gal 5:22-25)

We Will Know and Understand God and His Will, Ways, Plan and Purposes for Our Life in Our Heart by the Indwelling Holy Spirit:[2]The Spirit of the LORD shall rest upon Him, the Spirit of wisdom and understanding, the Spirit of counsel and might, the Spirit of knowledge and of the fear of the LORD. [3]His delight is in the fear of the LORD, and He shall not judge by the sight of His eyes, nor decide by the hearing of His ears;(Isa 11:2-3) [17]The God of our Lord Jesus Christ, the Father of glory, may give to you the spirit of wisdom and revelation in the knowledge of Him, [18]the eyes of your understanding being enlightened; that you may know what is the hope of His calling, what are the riches of the glory of His inheritance in the saints, [19]and what is the exceeding greatness of His power toward us who believe.(Eph 1:17-19) Therefore [27]The anointing which you have received from Him abides in you, and you do not need that anyone teach you; but as the same *anointing teaches you concerning all things*, and is true, and is not a lie, and just as it has taught you, you will abide in Him.(I Jn 2:27) [26]Likewise the Spirit also helps in our weaknesses. For we do not know what we should pray for as we ought, but the Spirit Himself makes intercession for us with groanings which cannot be uttered. [27]Now *He who searches the hearts knows what the mind of the Spirit is, because He makes intercession for the saints according to the will of God*.(Rom 8:26-27)

Regulating Lively and Deadly Thoughts and Intents by Our Mind

Mind is one of the inner faculties of humankind that we invariably employ while we are still alive. It is a tuner that sets our thoughts and intents of our heart. This function facilitates our understanding to the knowledge applied to our heart. It also helps us to prepare plans in our heart to reach our goals. In other words, what we are mindful in our heart at a particular instant is set by our mind. We can call to mind images, words and songs from the past by stirring up our memory. We use pictures for images, letters for words and music for songs to stir up the mind by the way of reminder. Sometimes we are mindful of the appearance of others, words they said and the songs they sang. For they either positively or negatively influence our emotional reactions.

When we work on projects with other team members, we all strive to have the same mind. We make sure to have no other mind to help eliminate the stumbling in our endeavor as we run towards a common goal. We successfully accomplish the project if we are like minded toward one another, in regard to the plan and purposes of our leader. Similarly, Bible exhorts the believers to be like minded toward one another, according to our Lord Jesus Christ. If we choose to do, we will have the mind of Christ. As a result, all of us may work in harmony being like minded, having the same love, being of one accord and of one mind. This positions us to be perfectly joined together with the same mind in the Lord as one body. Consequently, we may easily accomplish God's will, plan, and purposes in the ways of God, as a corporate body.

On the contrary, we will have a debased mind, if we do not like to retain the knowledge of God. If we choose not to believe in Christ, nothing is pure even our mind is defiled. For the veil is taken away only in Christ to see God and His kingdom. If we do not believe, surely the god of this age has blinded our minds. As serpent deceived Eve by his craftiness so our mind gets corrupted from the simplicity that is in Christ. As a result, we become people of corrupt minds who resist the truth, disapproved concerning the faith. Having our understanding darkened, we indeed are alienated from the life of God. This condition causes us to be vainly puffed up by our fleshly minds. Consequently, we walk in the futility of our mind and conduct us in the lusts of our flesh by fulfilling the desires of the flesh and of the mind.

Gaining Your Ability to Interact with God

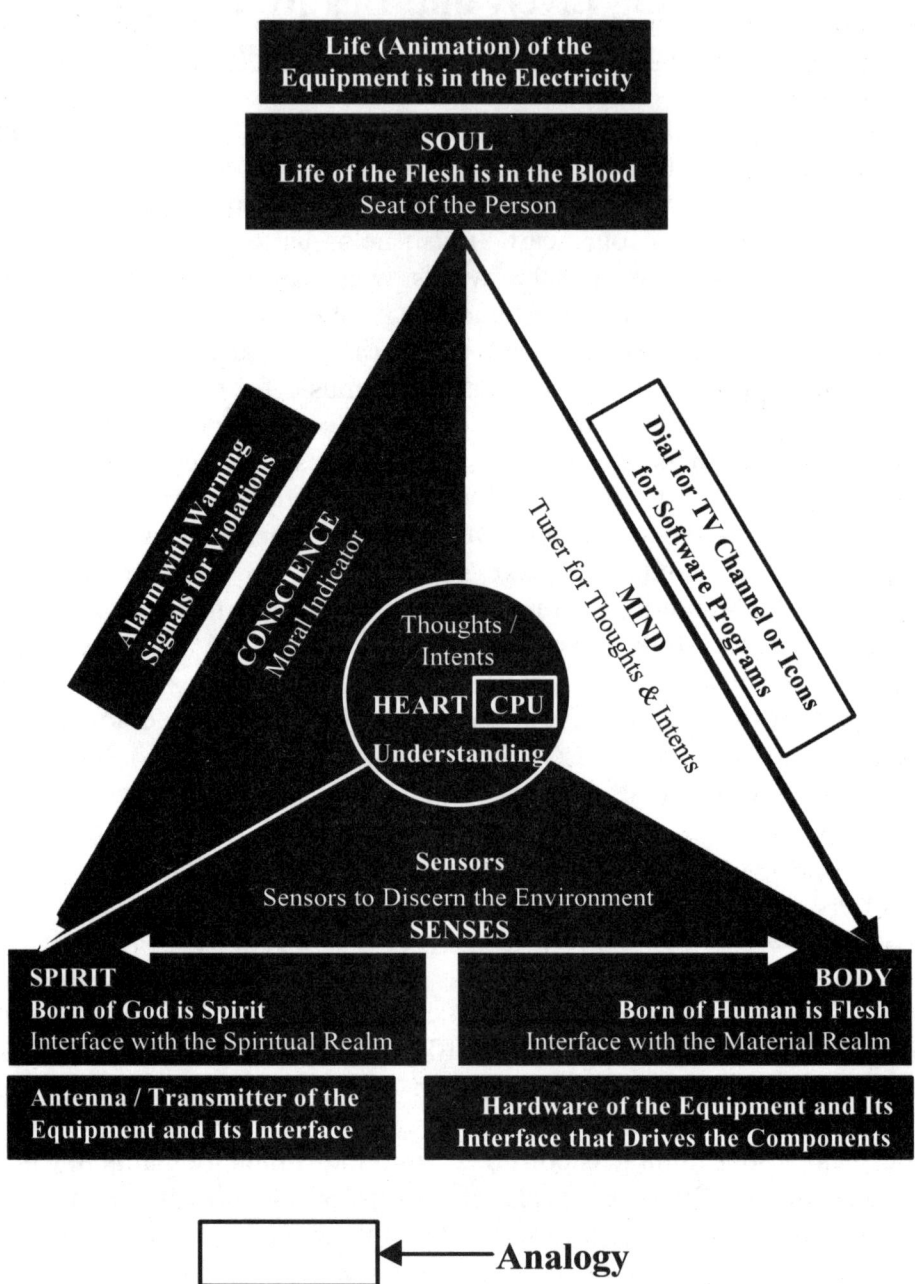

Analogy for the Mind of Humankind

Regulating Lively and Deadly Thoughts and Intents by Our Mind

The Bible says the laws are written in our heart and mind. This can be thought of as software programs stored up in the virtual and hard disk memories of a computer, respectively. The mind is like the icons of any equipment that employs computer, by which a particular program stored in the hard disk could be chosen and loaded to the CPU. Setting the mind to do something is like running the software program loaded to the CPU to find the answer. For these acts execute a logical sequence of commands built into the program. Similarly, focusing the mind on certain issue produces thoughts and intents in our heart in an effort to find solutions. This can be clearly seen in preparing alternate design plans, using our heart and mind. We invariably employ this to build something to fulfill a purpose of the owner. Typical examples include a house for living, a bridge to cross a river, cars to travel from one place to the other, ships to cross the ocean, planes to fly over the obstacles, rockets to go to other planets etc.

Mind also can be thought of as a tuner in any electronic equipment such as a TV. We set the tuner to a particular channel of our choice by the channel select button. Immediately, TV is filled with the light of the knowledge of the glory of the images, words and sounds (various noises and music) pertaining to that channel. Subsequently, they manifest through TV display and speakers. Similarly, we can set our mind basically on three primary channels known as flesh, world and heaven. Depending on our choice, our hearts are going to be filled with corresponding thoughts and intents. The things of the flesh are like the local information that comes through a TV from a video camera directly connected to it. The things of the world are like tuning into regular channels through an antenna that receives from a transmitter, which telecasts the information about the world. The things of heaven are like receiving information from another planet like moon using a satellite disc that manifests through a TV in a discernible form.

The visual summary for the make-up of human being together with the analogy is reproduced on the page to the left. The upper right triangular sector and the adjacent box pertaining to our mind are highlighted. The summary descriptions for the mind and the corresponding analogy within the highlighted area can be found inside the triangular sector and the adjacent box, respectively.

When we set our mind on the things of the flesh, we are filled with the images, words and sounds pertaining to the flesh. The data applied to the heart for understanding, in this case, is limited to our natural senses.

Gaining Your Ability to Interact with God

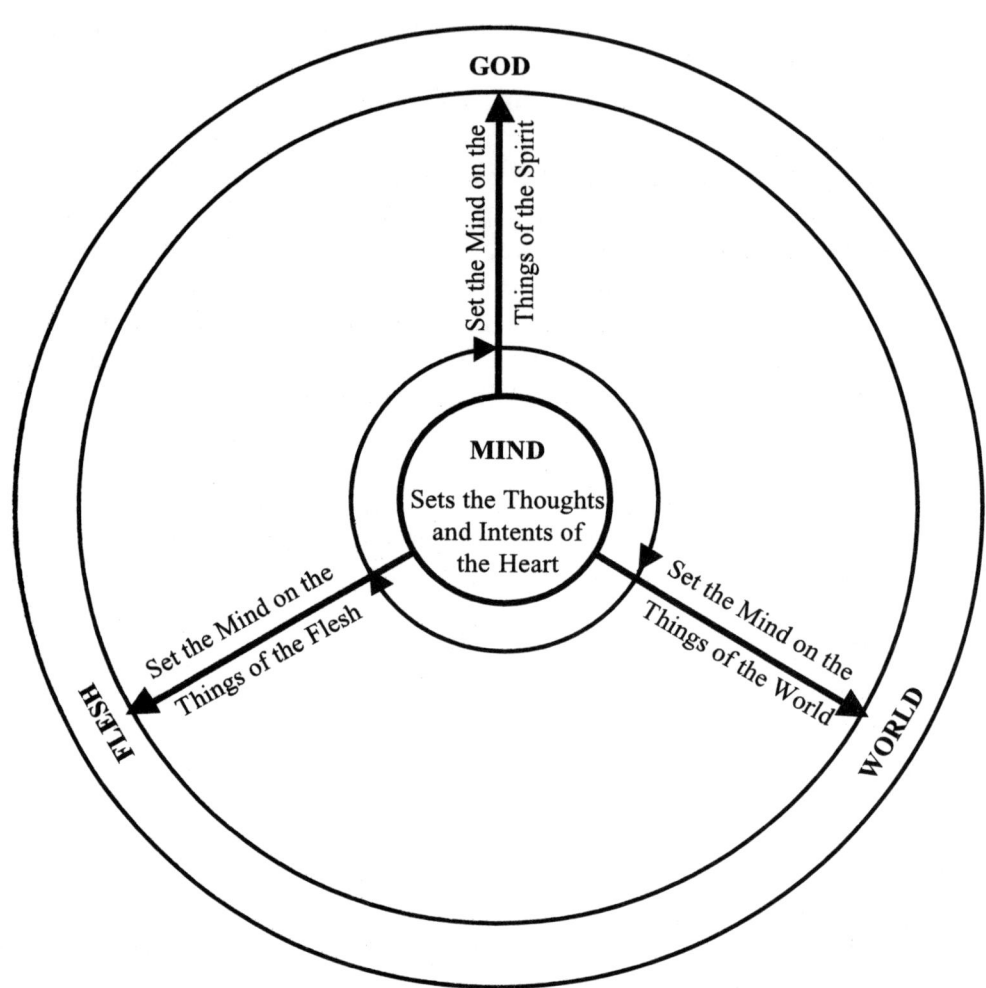

Three Different Settings of the Mind of Humankind

As a result, the plans that may be formed to fulfill the appetites of the flesh may be sinful. Because, the reasoning that goes in the heart is limited to the flesh and blood and does not acknowledge God and His laws. Finally, the choices we make to follow these plans both hinder our fellowship with God and cause us to abide in eternal death.

When we set our mind on the things of the earth, we are filled with the images, words and sounds pertaining to the desires of the world. The knowledge applied to the heart for understanding, in this case, is limited to the principalities, powers, rulers of the darkness of this world and spiritual wickedness in the spiritual realm. The pride of life, lust of the flesh and lust of the eye that fill our thoughts are of the world, not of the Father God. As a result, the plans of our heart to fulfill our appetites may be sinful. Because, the reasoning that goes in the heart is limited to the spirit of the world that is primarily rooted in pride, lust, fear of death and idols. The choices we make to follow these plans cause us to abide in the kingdom of darkness. Since the god of this world, the ruler of darkness comes to steal, kill and destroy, we may get destroyed and eternally die.

When we set our mind on the things of the Spirit, we are filled with the images, words and music pertaining to God and heaven. The knowledge gained and applied to the heart, in this case, is by the Spirit of God. The righteousness, peace and joy in the Holy Spirit may be a commonplace as we are filled with the Holy Spirit. The plans that may be formed in our heart to fulfill our appetites may be godly. Because, the reasoning that goes in the heart is primarily rooted in love and hope due to our faith on God's grace in Jesus name. The choices we make to follow these plans lead us to dwell in the kingdom of God. In other words, we may abide in eternal life owing to indwelling God who comes to give us an abundant life.

When we are separated from God either by sin or unbelief we do not have the inherent ability to be filled with the Holy Spirit. The natural man does not understand the things of the Spirit. Any amount of mental exercise is not going to help us to set our mind on the Spirit of God. In our analogy, we needed the satellite disc, the corresponding interface and programs in the CPU to discern what is coming in from another planet like moon. Similarly, things of God and His kingdom can be accessed only with a newborn spirit, a new heart and the indwelling Holy Spirit. In addition, we need the laws of God written in our hearts and minds to walk in the statutes of God.

A visual summary for various settings of mind is presented on page 102. As shown within the center circle, we proactively set the thoughts and intents of our heart by our mind. We can set our mind basically on three different things, as stated along three arrows radiating from the center circle. The thoughts pertaining to these settings of our mind inherently carry will, ways, plan and purposes that mutually contradict each other. For they, as shown along the outer circular annuls on page 102, are rooted either in God or the flesh or the world.

If we set our mind on things of the flesh, as shown on page 102 by the left downward arrow, the thoughts and intents that fill our heart are going to be confined to our natural senses. We may therefore have the appetites of the flesh and try to fulfill them in ungodly ways, according to the knowledge gained by our natural senses.

Alternatively, if we set our mind on things of the world, as shown on page 102 by the right downward arrow, the thoughts and intents fill our heart are going to be dictated by the spirit of the world. Consequently, we may have our appetites according to the knowledge of the world and fulfill them in ungodly ways.

On the contrary, if we set our mind on things of God by the Spirit, as shown on page 102 by the upward arrow, the thoughts and intents that fill our heart are going to be influenced by the things of heaven. We may know God and the things of God's kingdom. For we are empowered to see and hear through a newborn spirit and a new heart that provide access to heavenly throne by the indwelling Holy Spirit. We may therefore have desires from God that reflect His will, plan and purposes for our life. Moreover, we can choose to fulfill them in the ways of God by walking in fellowship with Him.

Bible References

The English translations for the Hebrew words **anamimnesko** ^363^, "to remind, call to remembrance"; **gnome** ^1106^,"a purpose, judgment, opinion,"; **dianoia**^1271^ lit. "a thinking through, or over, a meditation reflecting"; **ennoia** ^1771^ "an idea, notion, intent,"; **noema** ^3540^, "thought, design"; **Nous** ^3563^ "mind" the faculty of knowing, the seat of understanding; **sophroneo** ^4993^ "to be of sound mind" or one's right mind, sober minded; **hupomimnesko** ^5279^, "to cause one to remember, put one in mind"; **hupotithemi** ^5294^ "to place under" "risking the life" also denotes "to suggest, put into one's mind; **Phroneo** ^5426^ "to think, to be minded in a certain way"; **phronema** ^5427^ "to have in mind, to think, or an object of thought" are indicated by their corresponding Strong's numbers presented within parentheses as superscript in the Bible verses presented below.

Regulating Lively and Deadly Thoughts and Intents by Our Mind

Role of Our Mind in Storing, Recalling and Meditating Issues of Life

Our Minds Can Be Stirred Up to Recall Something Stored Up in Our Memory Either by Our Own Will or by Others: ⁶But one testified in a certain place, saying: "*What is man that You are mindful of him*, or the son of man that You take care of him?.(Heb 2:6) ¹⁵And truly *if they had called to mind* that country from which they had come out, they would have had opportunity to return..(Heb 11:15) ⁷²And a second time the rooster crowed. Then *Peter called to mind*⁽³⁶³⁾ *the word that Jesus had said to him*, "Before the rooster crows twice, you will deny Me three times." And when he thought about it, he wept..(Mark 14:72) ¹Beloved, I now write to you this second epistle (in both of *which I stir up your pure minds*⁽¹²⁷¹⁾ *by way of reminder*),(2 Pet 3:1) ³*Remember* the prisoners as if chained with them-- those who are mistreated-- since you yourselves are in the body also.(Heb 13:3) ????? ⁴greatly desiring to see you, *being mindful of your tears*, that I may be filled with joy,(2 Tim 1:4) ¹*Remind them*⁽⁵²⁷⁹⁾ to be subject to rulers and authorities, to obey, to be ready for every good work. (Titus 3:1) ²that *you may be mindful of the words* which were spoken before by the holy prophets, and of the commandment of us, the apostles of the Lord and Savior,(2 Pet 3:2) ¹⁵Nevertheless, brethren, I have written more boldly to you on some points, *as reminding*⁽³⁶³⁾ *you*, because of the grace given to me by God.(Rom 15:15)

Minding to Find Wisdom and Understanding (Meditation): ¹⁹Then Joseph her husband, being a just man, and not wanting to make her a public example, *was minded to put her away secretly*.(Matt 1:19) ⁹"*Here is the mind*⁽³⁵⁶³⁾ *which has wisdom*: The seven heads are seven mountains on which the woman sits.(Rev 17:9) ¹⁸Here is wisdom. *Let him who has understanding*⁽³⁵⁶³⁾ calculate the number of the beast, for it is the number of a man: His number is 666.(Rev 13:18)

Setting Our Mind for Team Work

We Can Have the Same Mind Among Ourselves by Walking by the Same Rule: ¹⁶Nevertheless, to the degree that we have already attained, let us *walk by the same rule, let us be of the same mind*⁽⁵⁴²⁶⁾.(Phil 3:16) ¹⁰I have confidence in you, in the Lord, *that you will have no other mind*;⁽⁵⁴²⁶⁾ but he who troubles you shall bear his judgment, whoever he is.(Gal 5:10) ⁵Now may the God of patience and comfort grant you to be *like-minded*⁽⁵⁴²⁶⁾ *toward one another, according to Christ Jesus*.(Rom 15:5) ¹¹Finally, brethren, farewell. Become complete. Be of good comfort, *be of one mind*,⁽⁵⁴²⁶⁾ live in peace; and the God of love and peace will be with you.(2 Cor 13:11)

We Can Be Perfectly Joined Together in the Same Mind for Good Things: ¹⁴But *without your consent*⁽¹¹⁰⁶⁾ I wanted to do nothing, that your good deed might not be by compulsion, as it were, but voluntary.(Phile 1:14) ¹⁰Now I plead with you, brethren, by the name of our Lord Jesus Christ, that you all speak the same thing, and that there be no divisions among you, but that you *be perfectly joined together in the same mind*⁽³⁵⁶³⁾ and in the same judgment.(1 Cor 1:10) ²I implore Euodia and I implore Syntyche *to be of the same mind*⁽⁵⁴²⁶⁾ *in the Lord*.(Phil 4:2) ²fulfill my joy by *being like-minded,*⁽⁵⁴²⁶⁾ *having the same love, being of one accord, of one mind*⁽⁵⁴²⁶⁾.(Phil 2:2) ⁶that *you may with one mind* and one mouth glorify the God and Father of our Lord Jesus Christ.(Rom 15:6) ⁸Finally, *all* *of you be of one mind*, having compassion for one another; love as brothers, be tenderhearted, be courteous;(1 Pet 3:8)

We Can Be Joined Together in the Same Mind for Bad Things: ¹³"*These are of one mind*,⁽¹¹⁰⁶⁾ and they will give their power and authority to the beast.(Rev 17:13)

Futility of Mind that Does Not Believe in God Through Christ

Minds of Unbelievers Become Futile for They Are Blinded to the Knowledge of God: ¹⁵To the pure all things are pure, but to those who are defiled and *unbelieving* nothing is pure; but even *their mind*⁽³⁵⁶³⁾ *and conscience are defiled*.(Titus 1:15) ⁴*whose minds*⁽³⁵⁴⁰⁾ *the god of this age has blinded*, who do not believe, lest the light of the gospel of the glory of Christ, who is the image of God, should shine on them.(2 Cor 4:4) ¹⁸*having their understanding*⁽¹²⁷¹⁾ *darkened, being alienated from the life of God*, because of the ignorance that is in them, because of the hardening of their heart;(Eph 4:18) ¹⁷This I say, therefore, and testify in the Lord, that you should no longer walk as the rest of the Gentiles walk, in *the futility of their mind*⁽³⁵⁶³⁾.(Eph 4:17) ²⁸And even as *they did not like to retain God in their knowledge*, God gave them over to a *debased mind*,⁽³⁵⁶³⁾ to do those things which are not fitting;(Rom 1:28) ³among whom also we all once conducted ourselves in *the lusts of our flesh, fulfilling the desires of the flesh and of the mind*,⁽¹²⁷¹⁾ and were by nature children of wrath, just as the others.(Eph 2:3)

People Whose Minds Are Corrupted Through Deception of Satan Resist the Truth: ³But I fear, lest somehow, as the serpent deceived Eve by his craftiness, *so your minds*⁽³⁵⁴⁰⁾ *may be corrupted* from the simplicity that is in Christ.(2 Cor 11:3) ⁸Now as Jannes and Jambres resisted Moses, so do these also resist the truth: *men of corrupt minds*, ⁽³⁵⁶³⁾ disapproved concerning the faith;(2 Tim 3:8) ⁵¹He has shown strength with His arm; *he has scattered the proud in the imagination*⁽¹²⁷¹⁾ *of their hearts*.(Luke 1:51) ¹⁸Let no one cheat you of your reward, taking delight in false humility and worship of angels, intruding into those things which he has not seen, *vainly puffed up by his fleshly mind*⁽³⁵⁶³⁾.(Col 2:18) ⁵useless wranglings of *men of corrupt minds*⁽³⁵⁶³⁾ and destitute of the truth, who suppose that godliness is a means of gain. From such withdraw yourself.(1 Tim 6:5) ¹⁴But *their minds*⁽³⁵⁴⁰⁾ *were blinded*. For until this day the same veil remains unlifted in the reading of the Old Testament, because the veil is taken away in Christ.(2 Cor 3:14)

If We Do Not Like to Retain the Knowledge of God, Our Mind Is Defiled and Leads Us to Be Engaged in Sinful Things Those Deserve Death: ⁶For to be *carnally minded is death*, but to be spiritually minded is life and peace. ⁷Because the carnal mind is enmity against God; for *it is not subject to the law of God*, nor indeed can be.(Rom 8:6-7) ¹⁵To the pure all things are pure, but to those who are defiled and unbelieving nothing is pure; but *even their mind and conscience are defiled*. ¹⁶They profess to know God, but in works they deny Him, being abominable, disobedient, and disqualified for every good work. (Titus 1:15-16) ²⁸And even as they did not like to retain God in their knowledge, God gave them over to a *debased mind*, to do those things which are not fitting; ²⁹being filled with all unrighteousness, sexual immorality, wickedness, covetousness, maliciousness; full of envy, murder, strife, deceit, evil-mindedness; they are whisperers, ³⁰backbiters, haters of God, violent, proud, boasters, inventors of evil things, disobedient

Regulating Lively and Deadly Thoughts and Intents by Our Mind

to parents, ³¹undiscerning, untrustworthy, unloving, unforgiving, unmerciful; ³²who, knowing the righteous judgment of God, that those who practice such things are ***worthy of death***, not only do the same but also approve of those who practice them. (Rom 1:28-32)

We Cannot Subject Our Mind to the Law of God Without the Help of the Holy Spirit: ¹⁵*If anyone loves the world, the love of the Father is not in him.* ¹⁶For all that is in the world-- the lust of the flesh, the lust of the eyes, and the pride of life-- is not of the Father but is of the world. ¹⁷And the world is passing away, and the lust of it; but he who does the will of God abides forever.(1 Jn 2:15-17) Therefore ⁵For those who live according to the flesh set their minds on the things of the flesh, but those who live according to the Spirit, the things of the Spirit. ⁶For to be carnally minded is death, but to be spiritually minded is life and peace. ⁷Because the ***carnal mind is enmity against God; for it is not subject to the law of God, nor indeed can be***. (Rom 8:5-7)

Life of God by Setting Our Mind on the Things of God

We Can Serve with the Mind the Law (Principles) of God: ¹⁰"For this is the covenant that I will make with the house of Israel after those days, says the Lord: *I will put My laws in their mind*⁽¹²⁷¹⁾ and write them on their hearts; and I will be their God, and they shall be My people.(Heb 8:10) ²³But I see another law in my members, warring against ***the law of my mind,***⁽³⁵⁶³⁾ and bringing me into captivity to the law of sin which is in my members.(Rom 7:23) ²⁵I thank God-- through Jesus Christ our Lord! So then, ***with the mind***⁽³⁵⁶³⁾ *I myself serve the law of God*, but with the flesh the law of sin.(Rom 7:25)

If We Set Our Mind on the Things of the Spirit and the Heaven We Will Have Life and Peace: ¹⁶*Be of the same mind*⁽⁵⁴²⁶⁾ *toward one another. Do not set your mind*⁽⁵⁴²⁶⁾ *on high things*, but associate with the humble. Do not be wise in your own opinion.(Rom 12:16) ⁵For those who live according to the flesh set their minds⁽⁵⁴²⁶⁾ on the things of the flesh, ***but those who live according to the Spirit, the things of the Spirit***.(Rom 8:5) ²*Set your mind*⁽⁵⁴²⁶⁾ *on things above,* not on things on the earth.(Col 3:2) ⁶For to be carnally minded⁽⁵⁴²⁷⁾ is death, but ***to be spiritually minded***⁽⁵⁴²⁷⁾ ***is life and peace***.(Rom 8:6)

We Can Be Renewed by the Spirit of Our Mind: Jesus said_²⁶"But the Helper, the Holy Spirit, whom the Father will send in My name, He will teach you all things, and ***bring to your remembrance all things that I said to you***.(John 14:26) ⁷For God has not given us a ***spirit of fear, but of power and of love and of a sound mind***.(2 Tim 1:7) ²⁶Likewise the Spirit also helps in our weaknesses. For we do not know what we should pray for as we ought, but the Spirit Himself makes intercession for us with groanings which cannot be uttered. ²⁷*Now He who searches the hearts knows what the mind of the Spirit is*, because He makes intercession for the saints according to the will of God.(Rom 8:26-27) ²²that you put off, concerning your former conduct, the old man which grows corrupt according to the deceitful lusts, ²³and ***be renewed in the spirit of your mind,*** ²⁴and that you put on the new man which was created according to God, in true righteousness and holiness.(Eph 4:22-24)

We Can Have the Mind of Christ and Cease to Sin: ¹⁴But the natural man does not receive the things of the Spirit of God, for they are foolishness to him; nor can he know them, because they are spiritually discerned. ¹⁵But he who is spiritual judges all things, yet he himself is rightly judged by no one. ¹⁶For "who has known the mind of the Lord that he may instruct Him?" But **we have the mind of Christ**.(1 Cor 2:14-16) ¹Therefore, since Christ suffered for us in the flesh, **arm yourselves also with the same mind, for he who has suffered in the flesh has ceased from sin**, ²that he no longer should live the rest of his time in the flesh for the lusts of men, but for the will of God.(1 Pet 4:1-2) Therefore ²***not to be soon shaken in mind*** or troubled, either by spirit or by word or by letter, as if from us, as though the day of Christ had come.(II Th 2:2) ¹³Therefore ***gird up the loins of your mind, be sober, and rest your hope fully upon the grace*** that is to be brought to you at the revelation of Jesus Christ; ¹⁴as obedient children, not conforming yourselves to the former lusts, as in your ignorance; ¹⁵but as He who called you is holy, you also be holy in all your conduct, ¹⁶because it is written, "Be holy, for I am holy."(1 Pet 1:13-16)

We Set Our Mind to Team Up with Others to Strive Together for the Faith of the Gospel: ²⁷Only let your conduct be worthy of the gospel of Christ, so that whether I come and see you or am absent, I may hear of your affairs, that you stand fast in one spirit, ***with one mind striving together for the faith of the gospel***, ²⁸and not in any way terrified by your adversaries, which is to them a proof of perdition, but to you of salvation, and that from God.(Phil 1:27-28)

Life of Death by Setting the Mind on Things of the Flesh and World

If We Set Our Mind on the Things of the Flesh and the Earth We Will Have Destruction and Death: ⁵For those who live according to the flesh ***set their minds***$^{(5426)}$ ***on the things of the flesh,*** but those who live according to the Spirit, the things of the Spirit.(Rom 8:5) ⁷Because ***the carnal mind***$^{(5427)}$ ***is enmity against God; for it is not subject to the law of God, nor indeed can be***.(Rom 8:7) ¹⁹whose end is destruction, whose god is their belly, and whose glory is in their shame-- ***who set their mind***$^{(5426)}$ ***on earthly things***.(Phil 3:19) ⁶For ***to be carnally minded***$^{(5427)}$ ***is death,*** but to be spiritually minded is life and peace.(Rom 8:6)

We Who Do Not Have the Spirit Think and Make Fearful and Lustful Plans to Win: ⁷For God has not given us a spirit of fear, but of power and of love and of a sound mind.(2 Tim 1:7) ¹⁸There is no fear in love; but perfect love casts out fear, because fear involves torment. But ***he who fears has not been made perfect in love***.(I Jn 4:18) ¹²And they said, "That is hopeless! So we will walk according to our own plans, and we will every one obey the dictates of his evil heart."(Jer 18:12) ¹⁵This wisdom does not descend from above, but is earthly, sensual, demonic. ¹⁶For where envy and self-seeking exist, confusion and every evil thing are there.(James 3:15-16) ²in which you once walked according to the course of this world, according to the prince of the power of the air, the spirit who now works in the sons of disobedience, ³among whom also we all once ***conducted ourselves in the lusts of our flesh, fulfilling the desires of the flesh and of the mind***, and were by nature children of wrath, just as the others.(Eph 2:2-3)

Law Based and Love Prompted Conviction of Our Conscience

Contrary to God's will, the first man Adam and first woman Eve chose to eat of the tree of the knowledge of good and evil. As a result, they became conscious of sin and righteousness, according to the written law of God, which later came through Moses. We, who are Adam's descendants including those who do not have a covenant with God, show the work of the law written in our hearts. For our conscience bears witness, between our thoughts accusing or else excusing us as guilty or not guilty. We therefore by nature begin to do the things in the law, being convicted by our own conscience. For example, we render to all their due for the sake of our conscience: taxes to whom taxes are due, customs to whom customs, fear to whom fear, honor to whom honor.

We sin whenever we fall short of keeping God's commandments. We transgress, when we trespass the boundaries set by the word of God. Sin and transgression include worshipping and serving idols in place of God. The idols in our heart set a value system that distorts God given priorities for our lives. We, therefore, may have a guilty conscience, for either sin or trespass or activities that conflict godly priorities. We know in our consciences that all of our thoughts, speech and the things done in our body are going to an account. And one day in eternity, our entire lives will be revised and God will judge us all. He may punish or reward us, according to what we have thought, spoken and done. Sometimes, many of us try to escape the guilty conscience by giving gifts and sacrifices to God and people. These are treated as dead works in the sight of God and produce no lasting results. For we do not have in ourselves a way of escape from a guilty conscience.

We can discern and know the moral condition of others by our conscience. We therefore, by our conscience, monitor the conduct of others who are directly or indirectly connected to us in our society. This helps us to escape from those who boast in appearance and not in heart. A crime may lie hidden in the memory, and the pain of its guilt may be toned down with time until it is found out. The disclosure in turn subjects the conscience to other people's consciences that will cause someone to experience their guilt in all its magnitude once again.

We can be redeemed from a guilty conscience only through the blood of Christ. When we become new covenant partakers by faith, we make Jesus as the blood atonement for our sin. We receive a new heart,

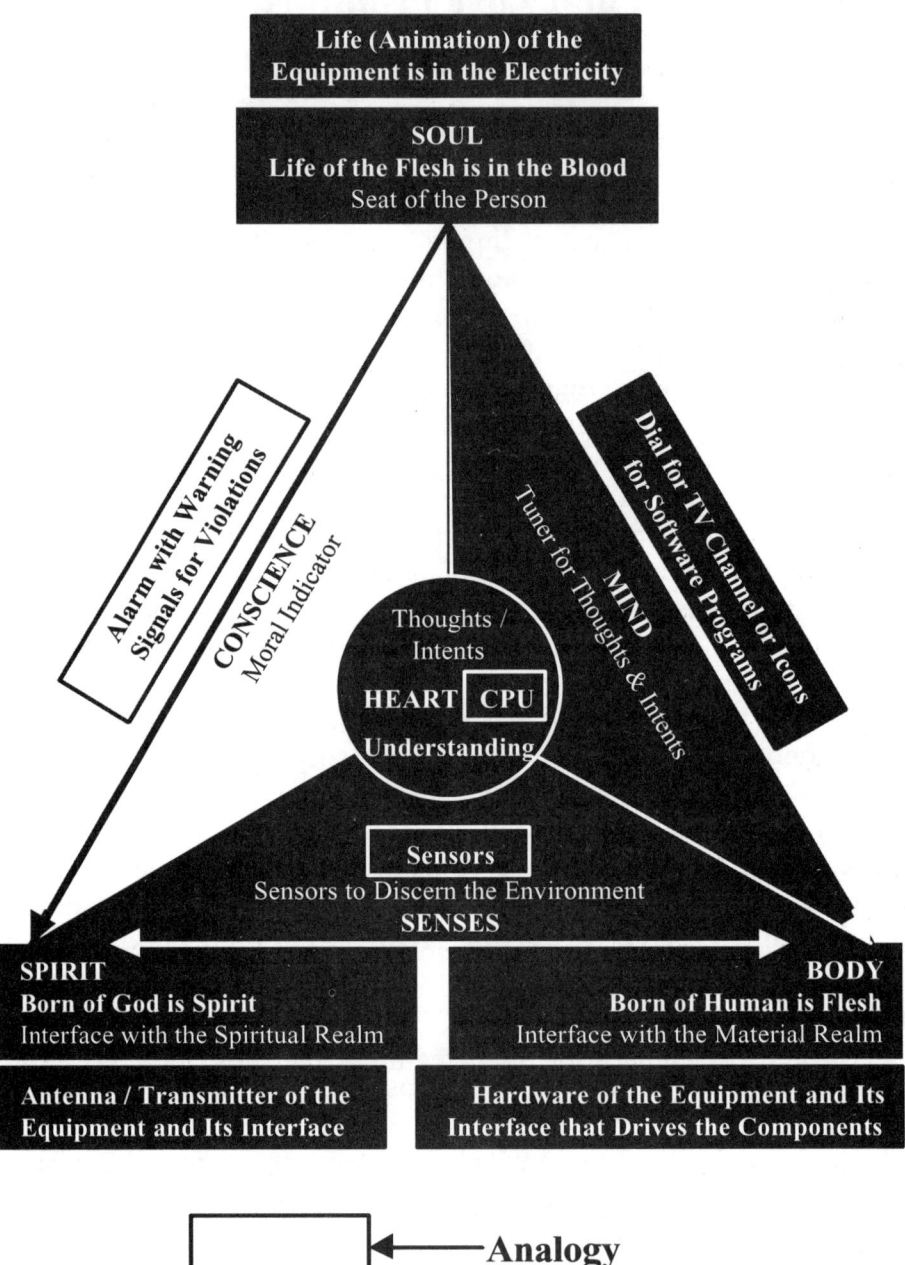

Analogy for the Conscience of Humankind

new spirit and the Holy Spirit within us and become one spirit with the Lord. The conscience therefore begins to bear witness with the Holy Spirit for love instead of right and wrong (good and evil). For the blood cleanses our conscience from dead works to serve the living God. Consequently, the guilty conscience that hinders our communion with God is no longer effective. This pardon and cleansing are entirely based on Christ as our atonement for our sin. Salvation in Jesus therefore enables us to be redeemed from the condemnation of our conscience as the blood cleanses us from all sin.

On the contrary, if we are defiled and unbelieving nothing is pure even our mind and conscience are defiled. We may readily yield to deceiving spirits and doctrines of demons and speak lies in hypocrisy. As a result, we lose our sensitiveness to right and wrong from God's perspective. For we have our own conscience seared with a hot iron.

The conscience is our moral indicator. It is like the alarm system that gives warning signals for violations in equipment, which employs computers. The warning system, which consists of hardware(alarm signals) and software programs loaded to the CPU, bears witness by monitoring the activities of the equipment. The CPU discerns the incoming flow of data as well as recognizes the ongoing operations. The warning system therefore monitors for the incoming data for validity and if necessary sets the alarm at this level. Also, warning signals come on whenever the operating conditions transgress the set limits. The alarm system essentially warns the owner/user for violating the regulations imposed either by the law or maker of the product. The error codes are displayed whenever there is something wrong in the operation. For example, when we drive the car the alarm signals come on to indicate things such as gas is low, oil is low, speed is higher/lower, temperature higher/lower, engine problems and so on.

The visual summary for the make-up of human being together with the analogy is reproduced on the page to the left. The upper left triangular sector and the adjacent box pertaining to our conscience are highlighted. The summary descriptions for the conscience and the corresponding analogy can be found inside the sector and the adjacent box, respectively.

Firstly, we consider the conscience toward self. First man rebelled against God and ate of the tree of the knowledge of good and evil. As a result, we humans gained the consciousness of good and evil by the conviction of our conscience for sin and righteousness. Once the conscience convicts of our sin, the gifts and sacrifices for God and

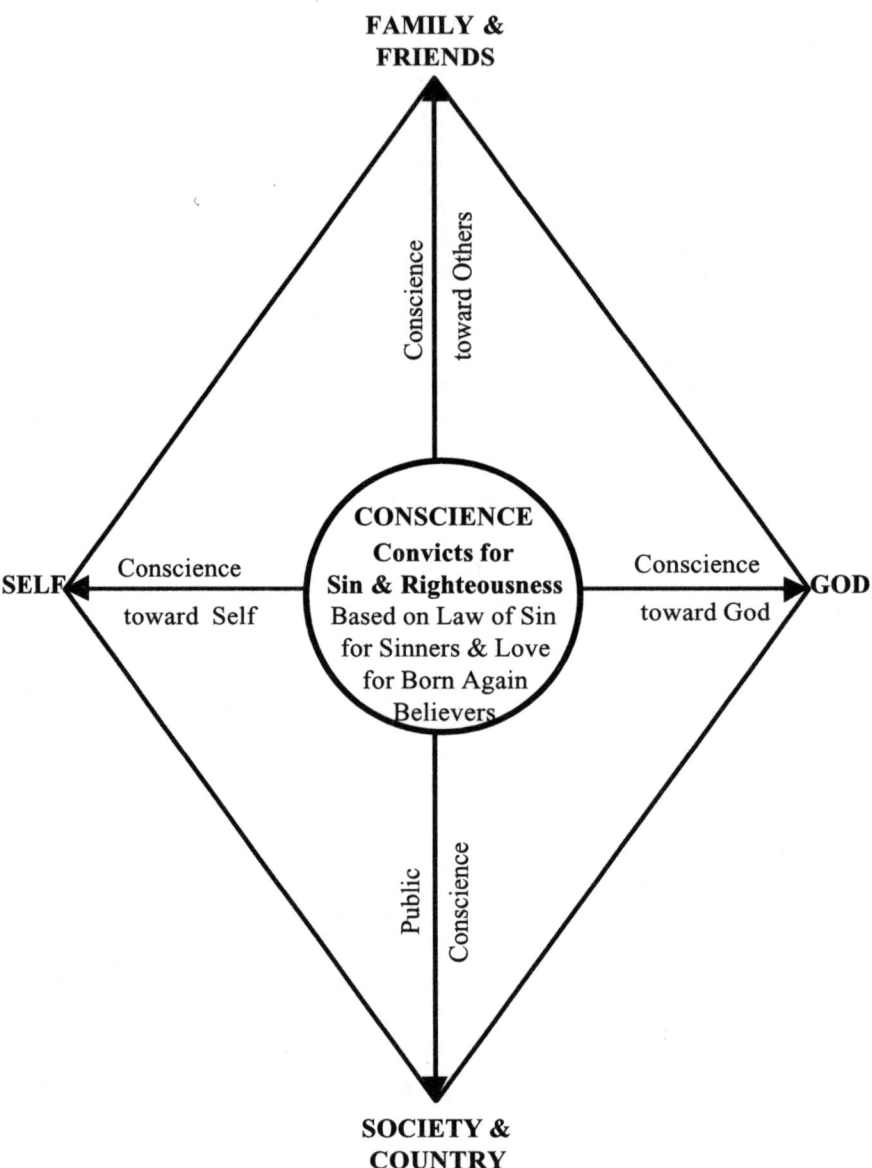

Conscience of Humankind Toward God and Others

people will not help us to get rid of a guilty conscience. We by nature therefore begin to do the things written in the law of God.

Secondly we may consider the conscience toward God. We all have guilty conscience toward God in one time or the other for all sinned. We however can repent by believing in the name of Jesus, for God made Jesus the blood atonement for our sin. The blood of Christ cleanses our conscience from dead works to serve the living God. A good conscience toward God bears witness in the Holy Spirit for love instead of right and wrong. When we live for Christ, we may face persecutions for the sake of our faith in the name of Jesus. A clear conscience toward God however sustains us while suffering wrong in the hand of worldly authorities. For we may not cast away our confidence in God to receive mercy and grace in times of need. We may therefore be able to pray for the enemies and walk in love even under oppression.

Thirdly, we consider the conscience toward family and friends. The members in our family and friends are the people directly connected to us in our daily life. If we are those who do not believe in Jesus, we basically stand right with each other according to our conviction of our conscience for right and wrong. In other words, we may invariably insist on our own rights in our relationships as a way of living. On the contrary, if we are those who do believe in Jesus, we basically stand right with each other according to our conscience that bears witness with the Holy Spirit for love. Consequently, we may not choose to do even those right things that cause others to stumble.

Fourthly, we consider the public conscience toward society and country. We judge by our conscience a number of people, especially those who do not directly associate with us, in the society and country. For example, the election process for government officials in a democratic system such as the president, senators, House of Representatives is essentially founded on the consciences of the voters. In addition, the court of law uses the voice of the consciences of jurors as the verdict for the convicts. In essence, we use the public conscience as a means of establishing justice and righteousness in our public affairs.

A visual summary is presented on the page to the left for the conscience of humankind toward God and others. Conscience, as shown inside the center circle, convicts for right and wrong based on the law of sin for unregenerate people and love for born again believers. We can have either a good (clear) or guilty conscience, as shown by four radiating arrows from the center circle, toward God; society and country;

self; and family and friends. The conscience convicts in regard to those shown at the corners of the quadrilateral on page 112 for sin and righteousness. It therefore helps provide judgment for moral issues at individual, social, political and family environments.

Bible References

The Moral Discernment by Our Conscience

We Are Conscious of Good and Evil Since First Spiritual Death: [16]And the LORD God commanded the man, saying, "Of every tree of the garden you may freely eat; [17]"*but of the tree of the knowledge of good and evil you shall not eat*, for in the day that you eat of it you shall surely die."(Gen 2:16-17) [4]Then the serpent said to the woman, "You will not surely die. [5]"For God knows that in the day you eat of it *your eyes will be opened, and you will be like God, knowing good and evil.*"[6]So when the woman saw that the tree was good for food, that it was pleasant to the eyes, and a tree desirable to make one wise, she took of its fruit and ate. She also gave to her husband with her, and he ate. [7]*Then the eyes of both of them were opened*, and they knew that they were naked; and they sewed fig leaves together and made themselves coverings.(Gen 3:4-7)

We Can Discern and Know Our Moral Condition by Our Conscience That Bears Witness Between Us and Our Thoughts: [12]For as many as have sinned without law will also perish without law, and as many as have sinned in the law will be judged by the law [13](for not the hearers of the law are just in the sight of God, but the doers of the law will be justified; [14]for when Gentiles, who do not have the law, by nature do the things in the law, these, although not having the law, are a law to themselves, [15]*who show the work of the law written in their hearts, their conscience also bearing witness, and between themselves their thoughts accusing or else excusing them*) [16]in the day when God will judge the secrets of men by Jesus Christ, according to my gospel.(Rom 2:12-16) [20]Therefore by the deeds of the law no flesh will be justified in His sight, for *by the law is the knowledge of sin*.(Rom 3:20)

We Can Discern and Know the Moral Condition of Others by Our Consciences: [10]For we must all appear before the judgment seat of Christ, that each one may receive the things done in the body, according to what he has done, whether good or bad. [11]Knowing, therefore, the terror of the Lord, we persuade men; but we are well known to God, and I also trust *are well known in your consciences*. [12]For we do not commend ourselves again to you, but give you opportunity to glory on our behalf, *that you may have an answer for those who boast in appearance and not in heart*. [13]For if we are beside ourselves, it is for God; or if we are of sound mind, it is for you.(2 Cor 5:10-13)

Day of God's Judgment in Eternity

God Judges Our Speech: [34]"Brood of vipers! How can you, being evil, speak good things? For out of the abundance of the heart the mouth speaks. [35]"A good man out of the good treasure of his heart brings forth good things, and an evil man out of the evil treasure brings forth evil things. ³⁶"But I say to you that for *every idle word men may speak, they will give account of it in the day of judgment*. ³⁷"For by your words you will be justified, and by your words you will be condemned."(Matt 12:34-37)

God Judges Our Works: ¹³Then I heard a voice from heaven saying to me, "Write: 'Blessed are the dead who die in the Lord from now on.'" "Yes," says the Spirit, "that they may rest from their labors, and *their works follow them*."(Rev 14:13) ¹²And I saw the dead, small and great, standing before God, and books were opened. And another book was opened, which is the Book of Life. And *the dead were judged according to their works*, by the things which were written in the books.(Rev 20:12)

God Judges Our Thoughts: ⁵Then the LORD saw that the wickedness of man was great in the earth, and that every *intent of the thoughts of his heart was only evil continually*. ⁶And the LORD was sorry that He had made man on the earth, and He was grieved in His heart. ⁷So the LORD said, "*I will destroy man whom I have created from the face of the earth*, both man and beast, creeping thing and birds of the air, for I am sorry that I have made them."(Gen 6:5-7)

Conviction of Sinners of the World by God

All the World Is Guilty Before God:¹⁸"There is no fear of God before their eyes." ¹⁹Now we know that whatever the law says, it says to those who are under the law, that every mouth may be stopped, and *all the world may become guilty before God*. ²⁰Therefore by the deeds of the law no flesh will be justified in His sight, for by the law is the knowledge of sin.(Rom 3:18-20) ¹⁴When Gentiles, who do not have the law, by nature do the things in the law, these, although not having the law, are a law to themselves, ¹⁵*who show the work of the law written in their hearts, their conscience also bearing witness, and between themselves their thoughts accusing or else excusing them*)(Rom 2:14-15)

Holy Spirit Convicting the World of Sin, Righteousness and Judgment: Jesus said ⁷"Nevertheless I tell you the truth. It is to your advantage that I go away; for if I do not go away, *the Helper* will not come to you; but if I depart, I will send Him to you. ⁸"And when He has come, *He will convict the world of sin, and of righteousness, and of judgment*:⁹"of sin, because they do not believe in Me; ¹⁰"of righteousness, because I go to My Father and you see Me no more; ¹¹"of judgment, because the ruler of this world is judged. (John 16:7-11)

Those Who Depart From Faith Lose Sensitiveness of Their Conscience and Error:¹Now the Spirit expressly says that in latter times some will depart from the faith, giving heed to deceiving spirits and doctrines of demons, ²speaking lies in hypocrisy, *having their own conscience seared with a hot iron*, ³forbidding to marry, and commanding to abstain from foods which God created to be received with thanksgiving by those who believe and know the truth. ⁴For every creature of God is good, and nothing is to be refused if it is received with thanksgiving; ⁵for it is sanctified by the word of God and prayer.(1 Tim 4:1-5)

Inability to Redeem from a Guilty Conscience Without God

Conscience of Unbelievers Is Defiled: *^{15}To the pure all things are pure, but to those who are defiled and unbelieving nothing is pure; but even their mind and conscience are defiled.* ^{16}They profess to know God, but in works they deny Him, being abominable, disobedient, and disqualified for every good work.(Titus 1:15-16)

We Cannot Make Us Perfect in Regard to Conscience and Free Us From Sin (Guilty) Consciousness Through Gifts and Sacrifices: ^{9}It was symbolic for the present time in which *both gifts and sacrifices are offered which cannot make him who performed the service perfect in regard to the conscience--* ^{10}concerned only with foods and drinks, various washings, and fleshly ordinances imposed until the time of reformation.(Heb 9:9-10) ^{1}For the law, having a shadow of the good things to come, and not the very image of the things, can never with these same sacrifices, which they offer continually year by year, make those who approach perfect. ^{2}For then would they not have ceased to be offered? For *the worshipers, once purified, would have had no more consciousness of sins*. ^{3}But in those sacrifices there is a reminder of sins every year. ^{4}For it is not possible that the blood of bulls and goats could take away sins.(Heb 10:1-4)

Cleansing of Our Conscience by Jesus Blood

Jesus Redeemed Us From the Curse of the Law by His Flesh and Blood: ^{4}But when the fullness of the time had come, God sent forth His Son, born of a woman, born under the law, ^{5}to redeem those who were under the law, that we might receive the adoption as sons.(Gal 4:4-5) ^{13}*Christ has redeemed us from the curse of the law*, having become a curse for us (for it is written, "Cursed is everyone who hangs on a tree"), ^{14}that the blessing of Abraham might come upon the Gentiles in Christ Jesus, that we might receive the promise of the Spirit through faith.(Gal 3:13-14) Jesus, ^{14} *who gave Himself for us, that He might redeem us from every lawless deed and purify for Himself* His own special people, zealous for good works. (Titus 2:14) ^{9}And they sang a new song, saying: "You are worthy to take the scroll, and to open its seals; for You were slain, and *have redeemed us to God by Your blood* out of every tribe and tongue and people and nation.(Rev 5:9)

Cleansing of Our Conscience by the Blood of Jesus From Dead Works: ^{6}But now He has obtained a more excellent ministry, inasmuch as He is also Mediator of a better covenant, which was established on better promises.(Heb 8:6) ^{24} to Jesus the Mediator of the new covenant, and *to the blood of sprinkling* that speaks better things than that of Abel. ^{25}*See that you do not refuse Him who speaks*. For if they did not escape who refused Him who spoke on earth, much more *shall we not escape if we turn away from Him who speaks from heaven*.(Heb 12:24-25) ^{14}how much more shall *the blood of Christ*, who through the eternal Spirit offered Himself without spot to God, *cleanse your conscience from dead works* to serve the living God? ^{15}And for this reason He is the Mediator of the new covenant, by means of death, for the *redemption of the transgressions under the first covenant*, that those who are called may receive the promise of the eternal inheritance.(Heb 9:15)

Law Based and Love Prompted Conviction of Our Conscience

Conviction of Believers' Conscience Based on Love

No Condemnation for Christ Believers: *¹There is therefore now no condemnation to those who are in Christ Jesus*, who do not walk according to the flesh, but according to the Spirit. ²For the law of the Spirit of life in Christ Jesus has made me free from the law of sin and death. ³For what the law could not do in that it was weak through the flesh, God did by sending His own Son in the likeness of sinful flesh, on account of sin: *He condemned sin in the flesh, ⁴that the righteous requirement of the law might be fulfilled in us* who do not walk according to the flesh but according to the Spirit.(Rom 8:1-4)

Our Conscience Bearing Witness in the Holy Spirit for Love: ⁵Now hope does not disappoint, because *the love of God has been poured out in our hearts by the Holy Spirit* who was given to us.(Rom 5:5) ¹I tell the truth in Christ, I am not lying, *my conscience also bearing me witness in the Holy Spirit*.(Rom 9:1) For ²²the fruit of the Spirit is love, joy, peace, longsuffering, kindness, goodness, faithfulness, ²³gentleness, self-control. *Against such there is no law.*(Gal 5:22-23) ¹⁷Now the Lord is the Spirit; and where the Spirit of the Lord is, there is liberty.(2 Cor 3:17) ²For *the law of the Spirit of life in Christ Jesus has made me free from the law of sin and death*.(Rom 8:2) Therefore ¹⁸if you are led by the Spirit, you are not under the law.(Gal 5:18)

Conviction of Conscience Prompted by Love Instead of Law of Sin and Death: ²³All things are lawful for me, but not all things are helpful; *all things are lawful for me*, but not all things edify. ²⁴Let no one seek his own, but each one the other's well-being. (1 Cor 10:23-24) ²⁸But if anyone says to you, "This was offered to idols," do not eat it for the sake of the one who told you, and for conscience' sake; for "the earth is the Lord's, and all its fullness." ²⁹"Conscience," I say, not your own, but that of the other. For *why is my liberty judged by another man's conscience?* (1 Cor 10:28-29) ³²*Give no offense*, either to the Jews or to the Greeks or to the church of God, ³³just as I also please all men in all things, not seeking my own profit, but the profit of many, that they may be saved. (1 Cor 10:32-33)

If We Wound Weak and Defiled Conscience of Others We Sin Against Christ: ⁶yet for us there is one God, the Father, of whom are all things, and we for Him; and one Lord Jesus Christ, through whom are all things, and through whom we live. ⁷However, there is not in everyone that knowledge; for some, with consciousness of the idol, until now eat it as a thing offered to an idol; and *their conscience, being weak, is defiled*.(1 Cor 8:6-7) ¹³*Therefore let us not judge one another anymore, but rather resolve this, not to put a stumbling block or a cause to fall in our brother's way.* ¹⁴I know and am convinced by the Lord Jesus that there is nothing unclean of itself; but to him who considers anything to be unclean, to him it is unclean. ¹⁵Yet if your brother is grieved because of your food, *you are no longer walking in love*. Do not destroy with your food the one for whom Christ died.(Rom 14:13-15) ¹¹And because of your knowledge shall the weak brother perish, for whom Christ died? ¹²But *when you thus sin against the brethren, and wound their weak conscience, you sin against Christ.* ¹³Therefore, if food makes my brother stumble, I will never again eat meat, lest I make my brother stumble. (1 Cor 8:11-13)

The Conviction of Our Conscience in Various Scenarios

The Conscience Convicts of Our Sin: ⁷So when they continued asking Him, He raised Himself up and said to them, "*He who is without sin among you*, let him throw a stone at her first." ⁸And again He stooped down and wrote on the ground. ⁹Then those who heard it, *being convicted by their conscience*, went out one by one, beginning with the oldest even to the last. And Jesus was left alone, and the woman standing in the midst. ¹⁰When Jesus had raised Himself up and saw no one but the woman, He said to her, "Woman, where are those accusers of yours? Has no one condemned you?" ¹¹She said, "No one, Lord." And Jesus said to her, "Neither do I condemn you; go and sin no more."(John 8:7-11) ⁹Then Joab gave the sum of the number of the people to the king. And there were in Israel eight hundred thousand valiant men who drew the sword, and the men of Judah were five hundred thousand men. ¹⁰And *David's heart condemned him* after he had numbered the people. *So David said to the LORD, "I have sinned greatly in what I have done; but now, I pray, O LORD, take away the iniquity of Your servant, for I have done very foolishly."*(2 Sam 24:9-10)

The Testimony of the Public Conscience Assures for Our Right Living: ¹²For our boasting is this: *the testimony of our conscience* that we conducted ourselves in the world in simplicity and godly sincerity, not with fleshly wisdom but by the grace of God, and more abundantly toward you.(2 Cor 1:12) ¹Therefore, since we have this ministry, as we have received mercy, we do not lose heart. ²But we have renounced the hidden things of shame, not walking in craftiness nor handling the word of God deceitfully, but by manifestation of the truth *commending ourselves to every man's conscience* in the sight of God. ³But even if our gospel is veiled, it is veiled to those who are perishing, ⁴whose minds the god of this age has blinded, who do not believe, lest the light of the gospel of the glory of Christ, who is the image of God, should shine on them.(2 Cor 4:1-4)

The Conscience Convicts in Regard to Fearing Authority, Paying Taxes, Following Customs and Honoring Whom the Honor is Due: ⁴And the men of David said unto him, Behold the day of which the LORD said unto thee, Behold, I will deliver thine enemy into thine hand, that thou mayest do to him as it shall seem good unto thee. Then David arose, and cut off the skirt of Saul's robe privily. ⁵And it came to pass afterward, that *David's heart smote him*, because he had cut off Saul's skirt. ⁶And he said unto his men, The LORD forbid that I should do this thing unto my master, the LORD's anointed, to stretch forth mine hand against him, seeing he is the anointed of the LORD.(1 Sam 24:4-6KJV) ³For rulers are not a terror to good works, but to evil. Do you want to be unafraid of the authority? Do what is good, and you will have praise from the same. ⁴For he is God's minister to you for good. But if you do evil, be afraid; for he does not bear the sword in vain; for he is God's minister, an avenger to execute wrath on him who practices evil. ⁵Therefore *you must be subject, not only because of wrath but also for conscience' sake*. ⁶For because of this you also pay taxes, for they are God's ministers attending continually to this very thing. ⁷*Render therefore to all their due: taxes to whom taxes are due, customs to whom customs, fear to whom fear, honor to whom honor*. ⁸Owe no one anything except to love one another, for he who loves another has fulfilled the law.(Rom 13:3-8)

Bibliography

Dr. Caleb K. Kabilamany *"Accessing God's Goodness for All Your Needs*, Living in God's Presence and Letting Him Restore His Glory Upon Your Life." Living Waters International Publishers, 2003.

Dr. Caleb K. Kabilamany *"How to Let God Flow through You*, Living, Moving and Having Your Being in God for an Abundant Life." Living Waters International Publishers, 2002.

Bibles and Concordances

King James Version.

New King James Version. Thomas Nelson, Inc., 1982.

New International Version. The International Bible Society, 1987.

The Comparative Study Bible. A parallel Bible presenting the New International Version, New American Standard Bible, Amplified Bible and Kings James Version. Zondervan Publishing House., 1984.

Cross References

Nave's Topical Bible., by Dr. Orville and Ann Nave.

Treasury of Scripture Knowledge., originally published about 1836.

Commentaries

The NIV Matthew Henry Commentary in one volume. Edited by Rev. Dr. Leslie F. Church. Revising Editor Gerald W. Peterman. Zondervan Publishing House. / Harper Collins Publishers Ltd., 1992.

Dictionaries and Encyclopedias

Nelson's Illustrated Bible Dictionary. Thomas Nelson Publishers, 1986.

International Standard Bible Encyclopedia (ISBE). Edited by James Orr and the Associates Dr. Edgar Y. Mullins and Dr. Johm L. Nuelsen.

New Unger's Bible Dictionary. Published by Moody Press of Chicago, Illinois. 1988.

Greek-Hebrew Sources

James Strong S.T.D LLD. *Strong's Exhaustive Concordance of the Bible together with Dictionaries of the Hebrew and Greek Words of the Original with Reference to the English words.* Riverside Book and Bible House. Originally published in 1894.

Interlinear Bible, Greek and Hebrew Transliterated Text

Word Study Reference Works

Vine's Expository Dictionary of Biblical Words (OT & NT), Thomas Nelson Publishers, 1985.

INDEX

A

Abundance...21, 22, 40, 60, 89, 90, 93, 114
Accusation 17, 27, 109, 114, 115
Alarm system 21, 22, 111
Alienation 27, 39, 46, 99, 106
Analogy........*See also* Word picture 18, 20, 21, 23, 43, 53, 54, 65, 77, 87, 101, 103, 111
Antenna 18, 19, 22, 43, 54, 77, 101
Application........17, 19, 71, 85, 94, 99, 101, 103
Atonement29, 79, 80, 82, 109, 111, 113

B

Baptism..........23, 36, 38, 43, 46, 60, 74
Bearing witness...17, 21, 27, 37, 38, 47, 49, 72, 109, 111, 113
Belief......19, 23, 27, 29, 37, 40, 50, 59, 62, 79, 83, 84, 87-89, 90, 95, 98, 99, 106, 113, 115, 118
Blood......15-20, 22, 35, 40, 53, 54, 57, 59, 65, 66, 72, 73, 75, 77, 80-82, 109, 111, 113, 116
Body......15-20, 22, 24, 30-38, 40, 41, 48, 49, 51-62, 63, 65, 67, 69, 74-83, 85, 96, 99, 105, 109, 114
   physical body 19, 52, 56
   possession 19, 29, 56
Bondage..............................23, 47, 49
Born
   of God......16-20, 30, 35, 36, 41, 43, 46, 63, 79
   of human..................... 16, 17, 20, 30
   of the flesh .16-18, 41, 47, 49, 51, 80
   of the Spirit....16, 17, 19, 20, 35, 36, 38, 41, 47, 49, 79
Boundary 24, 25, 109
Brain.. 15, 75
Bread..15, 17, 58, 60, 66, 73, 82, 95, 97
Breath......25, 31, 41, 46, 51, 57, 63, 65, 66, 69, 71, 73, 74, 75
Breath of the Almighty...25, 31, 41, 46, 66, 68, 69, 73, 74

C

Channel...........................21, 22, 101
Characteristic 17, 31, 38, 45, 46, 85, 88
Children..22, 25, 35, 40, 47, 49, 50, 61, 72, 80, 89, 90, 91, 106, 108
Choice...15, 17, 19, 21, 25, 27, 30-33, 37, 41, 53-57, 67, 75, 80, 85, 87, 90, 99, 101-104, 113
Christ.....18, 29, 37-40, 45, 48, 50, 51, 55, 59-62, 66, 71-73, 79, 83, 96-99, 105-109, 111, 113, 114, 116-118
Circumcision............. 35, 38, 90-92, 96
Circumstance 30, 33, 45, 67
Commandment...18, 21, 27, 48, 57, 62, 73, 85, 87, 94, 101, 114
Component... 18, 19, 21, 37, 53, 65, 77
Computer...18, 21, 22, 37, 53, 85, 101, 111
Condemnation.....23, 29, 40, 111, 115, 117, 118
Conscience... 15-18, 21-25, 27, 28, 37-39, 62, 75, 106, 109-118
   clear... 113
   good..................................35, 113
   guilty.................... 21, 109, 111, 113
Consciousness.......15, 24, 27, 75, 109, 111, 116, 117
Control. ...19, 29-31, 33, 54, 55, 57, 97
Conviction.......21, 23, 25, 27, 29, 109, 111, 113, 118
CPU (Central processing unit)... 18-22, 37, 65-67, 69, 77, 85, 87, 101, 103, 111
Creation...15, 22, 37, 38, 41, 50, 74, 79, 91, 107, 115
Creator........................... 22, 39, 46, 96
Creatures................................... 22, 91

D

Darkness.......29, 45, 47, 50, 55, 66, 69, 73, 77, 79, 103
Dealing 21, 34, 81
Death......15, 21, 27, 30, 31, 35, 37, 40, 41, 43-46, 48-51, 53-55, 58-61, 63,

121

66, 73, 75, 79, 80, 82-84, 94, 96, 103, 106, 107-109, 111, 113-116
Deeds.... 22, 30, 31, 34, 37, 38, 43, 55, 57, 59, 60, 114, 115
Delight 31, 98, 106
Deliverance 23, 97, 118
Demon....30, 39, 51, 54, 60, 62, 89, 90, 111, 115
Descendant 27, 96, 109
Desire.... 22-26, 31, 33, 40, 61, 89, 98, 99, 103, 104, 106, 108
Destination 15, 77, 80
Destiny 25, 40, 80, 87
Destruction...... 30, 47, 51, 80, 103, 108
Development 22, 23, 25, 27, 51
Devil 33, 88-90, 95
Devotion 23
Dial 21, 22
Discernment..15, 17, 19, 22, 38, 43, 45, 65, 67, 75, 77, 87, 103, 109, 111
Display.21, 29, 31, 55, 67, 69, 101, 111
Doctrine 39, 62, 89, 97, 111, 115
Dominion 27, 29, 30, 41, 45, 60, 97
Drink.15, 17, 25, 27, 33, 48, 51, 59, 60, 63, 65, 66, 73, 74, 82, 93, 116
Dwelling..... 18, 19, 23, 25, 35, 37, 38, 55, 59, 60, 74, 81, 82

E

Ears ...15, 31, 63, 69-72, 75, 94, 95, 98
Earth..15, 40, 41, 46, 49, 51, 53, 57, 58, 59, 66, 74, 75, 77, 80, 81, 93, 103, 107, 115-117
Electricity 18, 19, 22, 75, 77
Electronic equipment.....18, 19, 37, 53, 75, 101
Embodiment 17, 66, 89
Emotion...15, 17, 19, 27, 33, 34, 43, 75, 80, 85, 87, 90, 91, 99
Empowerment 23, 37, 104
Enemy 30, 33, 81, 94, 95, 113, 118
Environment . 22, 25, 33, 63, 65, 66, 67
  natural 17, 18, 63
  spiritual and natural 19
Equipment....18, 19, 21, 22, 37, 53, 54, 65, 75, 77, 85, 101, 111

Eternal Life...18, 25, 34, 37, 41, 45, 48, 59, 60, 63, 66, 69, 71, 72, 74, 79, 82, 83, 103
Eternity 15, 79, 109
Evil
  conscience 27, 35
  leaders 30, 32
  spirits 19, 29, 51, 54-57, 63
Excuse 17, 27, 109, 114, 115
Experience 23, 109
Eye...15, 27, 45, 48, 50, 55, 58, 63, 67, 71, 72, 75, 94, 98, 114, 115

F

Face...15, 21, 35, 45, 49, 58, 66, 73, 85, 93, 113, 115
Faculty 21, 26, 29, 99
Faith. 22, 25, 29, 30, 31, 35, 37-41, 43, 45, 48, 50, 61, 71, 79, 83, 84, 87, 89, 91, 97, 99, 103, 106, 108, 109, 113, 115, 116
Family 34, 51, 67, 113, 114
Father.....17, 29, 30, 37, 41, 45, 47-50, 59-61, 67, 72, 74, 81, 82, 95, 98, 103, 105, 107, 115, 117
Fear...17, 30, 31, 45, 47, 49, 50, 73, 75, 77, 79, 83, 85, 89-91, 95, 98, 103, 106-109, 115, 118
  of death 31, 79, 89, 91, 103
  of God..... 30, 31, 45, 79, 89, 91, 115
  of people 90
Fellowship. 23, 24, 30, 34, 37, 45, 103, 104
Flesh..... 15-21, 23, 25, 29-31, 33, 35, 40, 41, 46, 48-51, 54-61, 63, 65, 66, 67, 72-75, 77, 80-82, 90, 91, 94-99, 101-104, 106-108, 114, 115, 117
Flesh and blood...15, 18, 40, 58, 66, 72, 77, 80, 81, 103
Follow....... 19, 33, 62, 69, 71, 103, 115
Food......15, 17, 24, 25, 27, 33, 51, 53, 60, 63, 65, 66, 71, 74, 81, 82, 87, 94, 114, 117
Forgiveness 21, 29
Freewill Choice...15, 17, 21, 30, 32, 33, 53, 75, 78, 80, 85
Fruits 15, 60, 89, 90

Index

Fulfillment...19, 22, 25, 31, 40, 61, 99, 106, 108
Function. 18, 19, 21, 22, 43, 46, 53, 54, 57, 75, 99

G

Garden 27, 57, 114
Gifts and sacrifices ... 21, 109, 111, 116
God
   is light............. 27, 28, 37, 69, 73, 91
   is love..................... 27, 28, 37, 91
   is Spirit 17, 27, 28, 35
   is word 27, 28, 37
   of this world .. 21, 30, 33, 54, 55, 103
   the Father 28, 29, 41, 60
   the Son 28, 29
Godhead.................. 23, 28, 29, 37, 46
Government 30, 67, 75, 113
Grace. 22, 25, 34, 41, 45, 50, 60, 82, 83, 87, 89, 93, 96, 97, 103, 105, 108, 113, 118

H

Hardware 19, 22, 37, 53, 77, 111
Health 24, 25, 65
Hearing...53, 61, 63, 65, 68-73, 83, 84, 89, 97, 98
Heart..... 15-21, 25, 31, 34, 35, 38-50, 53-55, 59, 63, 65-72, 74, 75, 79, 81, 83, 84, 85-98, 99, 101-104, 106, 108, 109, 114, 115, 118
   new heart.... 23, 35, 37, 38, 40, 48, 49, 55, 63, 69, 71, 72, 77, 79, 91, 97, 103, 104, 109
Heaven... 15, 18, 29, 30, 35, 37, 43, 46, 49, 50, 54, 58, 59, 66, 72, 73, 75, 77-81, 83, 84, 94, 101, 103, 104, 115, 116
Hell................. 15, 40, 51, 75, 78-80, 83
Holiness 25, 28, 36, 50, 59, 105, 108
Holy Spirit... 19, 23, 28, 29, 31, 35-39, 41, 43, 45, 46, 49, 51, 54, 55, 57, 59-61, 63, 67-69, 71, 72, 74, 79, 84, 90, 91, 96-98, 103, 104, 107, 111, 113, 115, 117
Hope....... 30, 31, 50, 79, 89, 91, 94, 98, 103, 108, 117
Humankind...15, 21, 26-29, 32, 33, 40-44, 51, 54, 56, 65, 69, 70, 77, 78, 85, 87, 99, 101, 111, 113
Humility............................ 17, 45, 106
Husband.......... 22, 27, 48, 79, 105, 114

I

Identify 15, 43, 46
Idol...23, 24, 31, 48, 77, 79, 89-91, 97, 103, 109, 117
Image.... 15, 18, 19, 21, 39, 43, 51, 58, 67, 69, 71, 73, 75, 77, 90, 91, 96, 99, 101, 103, 106, 116, 118
Impartation............................... 19, 22
Indwelling... 23, 28, 29, 36-38, 56, 63, 79, 89, 103, 104
Infilling............................ 19, 36, 56
Information........ 15, 17, 18, 22, 37, 43, 54, 57, 69, 71, 75, 90, 91, 101
Inheritance 22, 50, 98, 116
Instruction...................... 19, 85, 87, 94
Intent..... 17, 18, 21, 22, 31, 55, 87, 89-91, 93, 99, 101, 104
Interaction... 15, 17, 18, 19, 22, 29, 30, 37, 38, 43, 46, 54, 57, 91
   ability......................... 15, 19, 27, 38
   with God 18, 38
Interface....... 15-22, 34, 37, 43, 46, 54, 57, 103
Issues of life....... 15, 18, 19, 30, 33, 85, 87, 91, 93

J

Jesus
   blood.......................... 21, 25, 63, 71
   name 29, 40, 51, 103
   Son of God 23, 73, 74, 83, 89, 90
Judgment.......29, 39, 40, 45, 49, 73, 79, 84, 95, 98, 104, 105, 107, 109, 113-115, 117

K

Kingdom..... 17, 18, 25, 29, 30, 32, 35, 37, 40, 41, 43, 45, 47, 49, 58, 60-63, 69, 71-73, 75, 77-81, 89-91, 95, 98, 99, 103, 104
   of darkness 30, 32, 78, 79, 80, 103

of God... 17, 18, 25, 32, 40, 41, 45, 47, 49, 58, 60-63, 72, 73, 77-79, 80, 81, 90, 91, 98, 103
Knowledge...17-19, 23, 24, 27, 30, 39, 43, 47, 50, 58, 67-69, 71, 77, 85, 87, 90, 94, 98, 99, 103, 104, 106, 109, 111, 114, 115, 117
- of good and evil.....27, 58, 109, 111, 114
- of sin.............................27, 114, 115
- of the truth................ 23, 83, 84, 115

L

Law
- curse of the law 30, 97, 116
- in the heart 88, 89
- of love.. 23
- of sin and death 23, 27, 59, 117

Leader................30, 33, 54, 55, 57, 99
- Lead....... 19, 21, 37, 47-49, 103, 117
- Leadership........................19, 30, 31
- political................................. 22, 30

Liberty 23, 84, 117

Life
- abundant 26, 31, 33, 103
- eternal ....See Eternal life
- in the flesh.......25, 33, 63, 65, 71, 75
- in the spirit....25, 29, 31, 33, 63, 65, 66, 71, 75, 79
- of the flesh.....15-17, 19, 20, 22, 57, 75, 80, 82
- physical................ 15, 25, 51, 56, 63
- spiritual..................... 25, 36, 44, 68

Light
- of life.. 18, 19, 27-29, 37, 44, 45, 63, 68, 69, 73
- of the knowledge.. 18, 43, 67, 69-71, 73, 77, 90, 91, 101

Logical sequence................21, 85, 101
Lost......... 27, 29, 37, 38, 40, 43, 77, 82
Lost condition 27, 29, 37, 40, 43, 77
Love.. 17-19, 22, 27-31, 35-38, 44, 45, 50, 55, 61, 63, 67, 71, 79, 83-85, 87, 89, 91, 93, 95, 96, 98, 99, 103, 105, 107, 108, 111-113, 117, 118
Love for life..18, 19, 27-29, 37, 44, 45, 63

Lust...19, 29, 31, 59, 61, 77, 79, 89, 90, 91, 95, 103, 107
- of the eye......................29, 103, 107
- of the flesh...19, 29, 59, 61, 95, 103, 107

M

Make-up...15-17, 21, 43, 53, 54, 65, 77, 87, 101, 111
Material *See also* Realm (material) .. 22
Meditation.........19, 31, 48, 85, 94, 104
Mercy 27, 34, 41, 45, 48, 113, 118
Mind..15-18, 20-22, 24, 25, 28, 36-39, 50, 54, 55, 61, 75, 91, 97, 98, 99-108, 111, 114, 116
Mirror 15, 18, 21, 85, 87
Mission 24, 25
Monitor.............................. 18, 19, 111
Morality
- indicator............16, 18, 20, 110, 111
- issues 17, 109-118
- laws..............................23, 109-111
Motivation 22-25, 30, 31, 77
Mouth....15, 17, 31, 40, 41, 46, 54, 55, 57, 65, 69, 71, 75, 81, 82, 84, 87-90, 93, 94, 105, 114, 115
Mouth of God............................ 17, 82
Music.....18, 21, 43, 63, 71, 90, 91, 99, 101, 103

N

Name of the Lord 21, 84
Noise.. 90, 93

O

Obedience 31
Obstacle 25, 101
Operation 18, 19, 21, 22, 23, 43, 111
Operator.................. 18, 19, 22, 37, 85
Oppression............................31, 113
Organization 22, 25
Output....................................... 21, 85
Overcome................. 19, 25, 41, 50, 55
Owner... 22

P

Parent.......... 19, 22, 25, 30, 41, 51, 107

Index

Patience 25, 89, 105
Person....15, 17, 37, 40, 45, 50, 51, 57, 73, 75, 85
Personal lordship........................ 30-32
Plan...24, 25, 30, 31, 37, 38, 41, 51, 54, 55, 57, 63, 90, 99, 104
Potential........................ 25, 31, 33, 51
Power......17, 31, 35, 39, 41, 43, 45, 46, 50, 55, 58, 61, 73, 74, 77, 81, 84, 90, 98, 103, 106-108
Pray....17, 30, 35, 38, 82, 98, 107, 113, 118
Preaching 29, 49, 84
Pride..17, 29, 31, 39, 45, 47, 77, 79, 81, 89, 90, 91, 96, 103, 106, 107
Principality........31, 55, 66, 77, 81, 103
Principle..........19, 25, 77, 85, 87, 89-91
Priority......................... 19, 23, 89, 109
Process......................... 17, 18, 77, 113
Program 19, 21, 37, 53, 77, 85, 90, 103
Property 22
Prosperity............22, 23, 26, 41, 87, 89
Purpose.. 30, 31, 35, 37, 38, 53-55, 57, 75, 90, 91, 93, 99, 101, 104

Q

Quench 23
Quest 23

R

Race.. 25, 89
Radio 18, 68, 71
Realm
  intangible 22, 46
  material....................... 15, 16, 20, 66
  of the spirit...... 17, 43, 66, 67, 69, 71
  spiritual....16, 18, 20, 31, 65, 69, 71, 103
  spiritual and natural 19, 71
Reason.............. 17, 49, 80, 85, 97, 116
Redemption.................. 27, 30, 40, 116
Reflection 19, 21, 85, 87, 93
Regulation.............................. 19, 85
Remote source................ 18, 22, 43, 77
Repentance................ 21, 34, 35, 66, 74
Response
  proactive 15, 30-33, 75, 80, 85
  proactive and reactive . 15, 19, 75, 80
  reactive...................... 19, 33, 34, 85
Righteousness...17, 21, 23, 27, 29, 37-39, 41, 50, 59, 60, 61, 77, 79, 84, 98, 103, 107, 109, 111, 113-115
Ruler
  of the darkness.......... 31, 77, 81, 103
  of this world.......................29, 115

S

Salvation.... 29, 35, 40, 49, 62, 63, 65, 73, 75, 83, 84, 94, 95, 108, 111
Sanctification 25, 60, 84
Satan.21, 27, 30, 33, 38, 39, 43, 54, 55, 57, 62, 66, 90, 91, 96, 97, 106
Scenario 21, 27, 34, 51, 77, 90
Seat of the person *See also* Soul...15-18, 20, 37, 54, 57, 75, 76, 78, 80
Secret.......................... 29, 45, 47, 114
Seed................................23, 60, 89, 95
Self......................30, 43, 46, 111, 114
Senses....15-18, 20, 22, 24, 30, 37, 53, 54, 57, 63, 65, 68, 70, 71, 85, 104
  natural....19, 25, 54, 70, 71, 89, 101, 104
  spiritual and natural 19, 64, 68, 69
  spiritual........... 17, 25, 29, 38, 63-65
Sensors 19, 20, 22, 53, 64-67, 75, 85
Separation 15, 17, 30, 45, 66, 75
Serpent.................27, 38, 99, 106, 114
Setting the mind......17, 21, 31, 55, 99, 101, 103-104
Sex..................................24, 25, 67
Sickness........................ 30, 33, 45, 49
Sight...... 23, 45, 50, 53, 63, 65, 68-71, 73, 85, 98, 109, 114, 115, 118
Signal for warning........ 21, 22, 85, 111
Sin....17, 21, 23, 27, 29-31, 34, 37-41, 48, 51, 58-60, 72, 75, 79, 82, 84, 97, 103, 107-109, 111-113, 115, 117, 118
Skill... 24, 25
Skin 15, 67, 71
Slavery... 23
Smell 15, 63, 65, 66, 71, 74
Society...................... 25, 34, 109, 113

Software program....21, 22, 53, 65-67, 85, 101, 111
Soul........... 15-20, 22-24, 28, 29, 31, 33- 37, 40, 51, 54, 55, 57, 75-82, 85, 91, 93, 96
Sound............. 19, 65, 71, 90, 101, 103
Spaceship... 18
Speaker....... 21, 22, 37, 43, 53, 85, 101
Speech....22, 30, 37, 38, 43, 45, 55, 57, 109
Spirit
　new spirit16-18, 20, 23, 24, 30, 35, 37, 38, 40, 41-50, 55, 63, 69, 71, 72, 77, 79, 91, 97, 103, 104, 111
　of life.. 18, 19, 27, 29, 37, 41, 63, 65, 66, 71, 74
　of the Father......................28, 67, 79
　of the Son..........................28, 67, 79
　of the world....29, 30, 33, 55, 57, 66, 79, 80, 90-93, 103, 104
Summary.*See also* Visual Summary 18, 26, 29, 43, 54, 77, 80, 87, 101, 111
Superimpose.........................21, 26, 29
Sustenance...15, 17, 25, 45, 49, 51, 63, 65, 66, 71

T

Taste............. 15, 37, 63, 65, 66, 71, 73
Team...............................99, 105, 108
Temperature......19, 53, 67, 77, 85, 111
Temptation.. 31
Things
　of God.......17, 21, 31, 38, 40, 43, 47, 63, 65, 69, 71, 72, 79, 89, 97, 103, 104
　of the flesh...17, 21, 31, 54, 61, 101, 104, 107, 108
　of the world...15, 17, 21, 31, 34, 63, 77, 101, 104
Thoughts...... 16-18, 20-22, 25, 27, 28, 31, 37, 38, 39, 55, 62, 86-93, 96, 99, 101-104, 109, 114, 115
Tongue...39, 47, 53, 62, 84, 91, 93, 94, 95, 116
Touch..................37, 65, 67, 71, 74, 82
Transmission..... 18, 19, 22, 31, 37, 43, 54, 77, 101

Treasure. 21, 40, 85, 89-90, 93, 94, 115
Truth......23, 39, 50, 60, 82, 83, 84, 91, 96, 98, 99, 106, 115, 117, 118
Tune 18, 22
TV (Television)...... 18, 21, 22, 37, 43, 67, 69, 90, 101

U

Unbeliever 28, 29
Uncircumcision.............. 90, 92, 95, 96
Understanding....15-20, 26, 31, 39, 45, 47, 50, 53, 66, 67, 69, 71-73, 85- 88, 91, 93, 94, 96, 98, 99, 101, 103-106

V

Values........................ 19, 24, 27, 87-90
Victory....................................... 25, 58
Violation..................... 21, 22, 23, 111
Vision 24, 25, 87, 89
Visual summary..16, 20, 24, 28, 32, 36, 44, 56, 68, 70, 78, 88, 92 , 102, 112

W

Walk
　in the flesh............ 31, 32, 54, 78, 80
　in the light..................................... 79
　in the spirit 23, 32, 41, 78, 79
Water distribution system 23
Waves..... 19, 22, 31, 37, 43, 54, 69, 71
Weed.. 88-90
Wickedness.......31, 39, 77, 81, 93, 103, 106, 115
Wife..................................... 22, 58, 79
Wisdom...17, 27, 39, 50, 55, 77, 87, 94, 96, 98, 105, 107, 108, 114, 118
Word of God....17, 23, 63, 66, 74, 82- 84, 87, 89, 90, 93, 109, 115, 118
Word of life... 18, 19, 27, 29, 37, 45, 63
Word picture......18-22, 37-38, 42-43, 52-54, 64-71, 75-77, 85-90, 100-101, 110-111
Work
　dead works 21, 109, 111, 113, 116
　of the law .. 17, 21, 27, 109, 114, 115
Worship..17, 23, 24, 30, 34, 39, 43, 89, 96, 106

How to Let God Flow Through You
Living, Moving and Having Your Being in God for an Abundant Life

This book will transform you to be a powerful child of God through whom God operates. Practical, thought provoking analogies, visual summaries and illustrations will help you to easily and quickly get established in God. Ample information for you to let your thoughts, speech and deeds be directed by God. This book is a cross between a friendly talk of a slide presentation and a unique reference resource. It will enrich your fellowship and personal knowledge of God and facilitate His flow through you. Order your copy today!

Here you will discover

- the light of life, spirit of life, word of life and love for life in you due to indwelling God
- the personality of God in you
- God is Spirit; God is light; God is word &love
- God in you is the fountain of living waters

And useful personal guidance to:

- get united to God through Christ Jesus
- know why there is life in Jesus name and blood
- enter into God's presence for a new life
- communicate with God in heaven
- make God of heaven your Father by new birth
- let God work wonders and miracles through you

Quantity discounts for 12 or more

A Great Gift! No-Risk, Money-Back Guarantee

YES, I want this book. Send me ____ copies at $7.75 each, plus $3.50 shipping and handling per book. (California residents please include $0.60 sales tax.) Allow 30 days for delivery.

Name ———————————————— Phone ————————————

Address ————————————————————————————

City/State/Zip ————————————————————————

———— Check/money order enclosed

Charge my ____ VISA   ____ MasterCard   ____ Discover   ____ AmEx

Card #———————————— Exp.———— Signature————————

Make your check or money order payable and return to Living Waters International Publishers, P.O Box 1208, Lake Forest, California 92609.

Or for faster delivery order online using your credit card or checkpay through Website: livingwatersip.com or fax your credit card order to (949)-215-0498.

Accessing God's Goodness for All Your Needs
Living in God's Presence and Letting Him Restore His Glory upon Your Life

This book will help you to increase your quality of living far beyond your imagination. Practical, thought provoking analogies, visual summaries and illustrations will facilitate you to enter into God's presence and live there by His mercy and grace. The book is formatted to be a cross between a friendly talk of a slide presentation and a unique reference resource. It will empower you to draw near to God and experience His goodness. Order your copy today!

This will be Available in January 2003

Here you will discover your
- saved soul to prosper in God
- new spirit and heart to know God
- Spirit filled body to live in God's presence
- cleansed conscience to draw near to God
- renewable mind to know God's will for you

And useful personal guidance to:
- enter into God's presence and live there
- recognize God's presence upon you
- position yourselves to be protected by God
- be delivered from fear, sin, sickness & devil
- find mercy of God for all your mistakes
- receive favor for all your needs

Quantity discounts for 12 or more

A Great Gift! No-Risk, Money-Back Guarantee

YES, I want this book. Send me _____ copies at $9.95 each, plus $3.50 shipping and handling per book. (California residents please include $0.77 sales tax.) Allow 30 days for delivery.

Name _____ Phone _____

Address _____

City/State/Zip _____

_____ Check/money order enclosed

Charge my ____ VISA ____ MasterCard ____ Discover ____ AmEx

Card # _____ Exp. _____ Signature _____

Make your check or money order payable and return to Living Waters International Publishers, P.O Box 1208, Lake Forest, California 92609.

Or for faster delivery order online using your credit card or checkpay through Website: livingwatersip.com or fax your credit card order to (949)-215-0498.